BENEDICT ARNOLD SLEPT HERE

JACK DOUGLAS' HONEYMOON MOUNTAIN INN

JACK DOUGLAS

Benedict Arnold
Slept Here

JACK DOUGLAS'
HONEYMOON MOUNTAIN INN

G. P. Putnam's Sons   New York

Copyright © 1975 by Jack Douglas

SBN: 399–11432–7

Library of Congress Catalog
Card Number: 74–16587

PRINTED IN THE UNITED STATES OF AMERICA

To the warm, wonderful people of the "Pine Tree" state—and especially to the residents of the lovely little village of Granby Lakes—in Furbish County, Maine—without whose insistent cooperation this book never would have been possible. Or conceivable.

CAST OF CHARACTERS

(Besides Jack, Reiko, Bobby, and Timothy)

(Not in alphabetical order or in order of their appearance)

Joseph F. Fulman	Lawyer
Goldie Renk	Lawyer
Emil LaBoute	Lawyer
Cordell Mews	Lawyer
Quincy Deal	Lawyer
Gertrude Hinkley	Real estate sales person
Richard N. Huckle	State Senator
Richard N. Huckle	Owner, Granby Lakes Power Company
Richard N. Huckle	Chairman, State Power Authority Board of Appeals and Complaints
"Fat Max" Collings	Village policeman
Earl Harkins	Village drunk
Tydings Herley	Assistant village drunk
Betsy Couzy	Informer
Harper Fundy	Rigged Laundromat owner
Jock Lee	Bartender
Mosher Parsonfield	Undertaker
Thomas E. Yates	Owner, Fungo Springs Golf Course
Old Mrs. Granby	Old lady
Egil Grimshaw	Fuckermother

"Egil Grimshaw is a Fuckermother."

—Timothy Douglas, age five

CHAPTER

1

ABRAHAM Lincoln's father once said, "When you can see your neighbor's chimney, it's time to move."

In Honansville, Connecticut, high on a windy hill where we lived, in a lovely house we had just finished building, I looked out of one of our thousand-dollar picture windows and counted seven neighbors' chimneys in plain view. I thought about what Abraham Lincoln's father had said, and realized that we were six chimneys behind schedule. Not that how many chimneys were visible had anything to do with it. It seemed that we moved every four years for some unaccountable reason. Maybe Dear Abby could have told us why, but I didn't ask her because years ago when I wrote to her regularly every week about sex (where I could get some?) not once did she take the trouble to answer and after a while my letters came back unopened and stamped "Addressee Unknown"—then finally, "Get lost—you crummy bastard!" It was a suggestion a crummy bastard could not ignore and I never wrote to Dear Abby again.

I wrote to Sarah Lee and she fixed me up with a nice Jewish girl who was passing (as a Filipino).

Most normal people, when they want to get away

from everything, go *south* to Florida—an area which was created by the Mackle Brothers—after God gave it up as a bad job. God just couldn't figure what the hell to do with *all those people!* Strange—with His great creative powers He never thought about condominiums. Or maybe He was busy with other matters, like sending a few bolts from heaven to scare the bejesus (the original spelling) out of Mohammed and Buddha, who had gone into business for themselves.

We never went south. We always went north, because it was cheaper, and less congested. In Florida, no matter what shopping center you chose, you'd always find yourself blocked at the checkout counter by a little old lady senior citizen, trying to make up her mind whether to try prune juice, Haley's M-O, or a chocolate-covered cherry bomb. Or all three.

We had spent a couple of years in the Northern Ontario bush, which we loved, but we felt that our children should go to school and find out for themselves that "a little knowledge is a dangerous thing after four years at Princeton," which is a direct quote from Woodrow Wilson, who gave up a good job at the university to become President of the United States.

After four years in Honansville, I had grown extremely restless and that's why Reiko, my little Japanese doll-wife, and our two sons, Bobby, twelve, a devotee of Kung Fu, and Timothy, five, who spent most of his waking hours dodging the kick of death from his older brother, plus screaming for his bottle of Mother Myerson's Apple Juice, which was made from freshly crushed, artificially flavored citric acid and vegetable-dyed recycled mountain spring water, found ourselves one lovely August morning traveling down the long hill into the far northern village of Greenville, Maine, which is an untidy little township on forty-three-mile-long Moosehead Lake.

"Why do they call it Moosehead Lake, Papa?" Bobby asked.

"Because it's shaped like a moose's head."

"Oh."

We were in search of the perfect place to live, where there would be no chance of seeing a neighbor's chimney, unless the Mackle Brothers suddenly switched from peeled pink stucco bungalows to A-frame ski lodges for senior citizens who would rather spend the autumn of their years in traction than play shuffleboard in the nude.

Somebody was selling an island in the middle of Moosehead Lake which sounded (in the ad) like a pine-tree-covered paradise.

"Well," Reiko said to Mr. Anson, the Greenville real estate man, as we sailed closer to the island, "it's covered with pine trees all right, but why are they all brown?"

"Oh," Mr. Anson said, not at all ruffled by this, "at this time of the year they always turn brown—all pine trees turn brown in August." I didn't bother to dispute this, but I knew from reading the Georgia-Pacific magazine spreads for years that it wasn't exactly the truth, and besides, the pine trees covering the island just happened to be spruce trees.

"How about spruce trees," I asked, "do they turn brown, too?"

"Oh, no—they stay green all year round."

This conversation set the whole tone for our visit to this island paradise. There wasn't one item in the ad which coincided with reality. The island had been described as surrounded by sandy beaches. If so, they were buried under immense boulders, and the "gently sloping contours" turned out to be hundred-foot cliffs, which would have been a constant source of worry to us about Timothy. Ever since he saw Peter Pan, he thinks *he* can fly, too—and maybe he can—eventually. He's already got something that looks like pinfeathers. We've never really paid much attention to him—maybe he's a flamingo. Genetics play dirty sometimes.

Nevertheless, even if the island itself had been perfect, the house that went with it had been slightly less. A stiff breeze, I felt, would blow it over and into the lake, and as we left the island, a stiff breeze suddenly roiled the placidity of the sparkling water. I heard a loud splash. Like a fool, I looked back and was turned into a pillar of salt substitute.

In Greenville, we bought a genuine Taiwan tomahawk at the Old Indian Trading Post, and set out again to find the perfect dwelling place, and surprisingly—we found it. Unfortunately, it wasn't for sale. Mr. Anson told us the story. It was owned by an eccentric old lady who was expecting Caesar Romero any day, and she refused to sell because she felt that Caesar wouldn't like the idea. Furthermore, Mr. Anson related, *why* she was expecting Caesar Romero—or anybody—was never explained, except that this dear old lady was supposed to be crazy, although I couldn't figure out why people thought so. Her relatives, so the story went, decided years ago that she *was* crazy and tried to have her committed to a mental institution, but through some bureaucratic foul-up, her relatives—all twenty-seven of them—had been put away instead, and the dear sweet old lady—who belonged to the vaginal-spray-of-the-

14

month-club, in anticipation of Caesar's arrival—remained as free as the wind. A beautiful carriage of misjustice.

Disillusioned by the world scarcity of perfect places to live, which was especially noticeable at Moosehead Lake, we headed back to Connecticut and our thousand-dollar picture-window view of seven chimneys.

"I like it better in Connecticut anyway," Reiko said. "There's always something to do there."

"Like what?" I wanted to know.

"Well . . . we can go to the movies . . . anytime we want to."

"Jesus H. Christ!" I said. "The Bijou in Honansville plays only Dean Martin movies! How many times can you see the same Dean Martin movies?"

"Dean Martin," Bobby said, "sold his ranch in California for a million and a half dollars."

"I know. I know."

"He sold it to some Japanese guy."

"What was his name?" Reiko said.

"Dean Martin," Bobby said.

"What was the Japanese man's name?" Reiko said, with some impatience.

"Hirohito," I said. "They couldn't beat us, so they're going to buy us—that is, if the Arabs will sell."

"That's a cheap joke," Reiko said.

"We're way up in northern Maine, now," I said. "I'm not going to waste any expensive jokes on a bunch of retarded raccoons and gift shop proprietors.

On the way back to Honansville, miles and miles beyond the lovely village of Rangeley, we stopped at a soup stain on our Texaco map which turned out to be a little place on the shores of another magnificent northern lake. As we sat eating our peanut butter and jelly

15

sandwiches in a charming miniature village park which overlooked the lake, we became more and more enamored of the quiet beauty and the permeating tranquillity which seemed to be part of this delightful little park and the village. We had no idea we were being hooked.

"What's the name of this place, Papa?" Bobby said. I unfolded my Texaco map and looked at the soup stain. "Granby Lakes," I said, "that's Granby Lake out there."

"Why do they call it Granby Lake, Papa?" Timothy wanted to know.

"Because it's shaped like a Granby," I said.

"I'm going to throw up," Bobby said.

Miss Hinkley, the real estate woman from the Egil Grimshaw real estate and insurance office, filled us in about Granby Lakes as we drove around.

It seems that Squire Granby, who was probably the first land developer in the new world, had acquired Granby Lake and the eight million square miles around it from the Indians for two jugs of Boone's Farm wine and a copper bracelet (to ward off the white man). King George III was the real estate agent in this transaction, and both the king and Squire Granby were quite satisfied with the deal, but from all reports, this was the last time anybody in Maine was ever satisfied with a real estate deal.

Squire Granby's satisfaction was considerably watered-down later when he found that no one in 1774 was too interested in purchasing a fifty-foot lot in Granby View Acres, which is what he called his eight million square mile development. This became a great concern to Squire Granby because to lay out the streets and name them all with such enticing names as "Blueberry Hill Lane" and "Wilshire Boulevard," etc., in eight mil-

16

lion square miles took up most of Squire Granby's afternoons. And all of his mornings. And sometimes his evenings, during which he used a candle to light his way, a yardstick to measure, and a charming young girl, who played the cello and wanted to learn how to lay out streets. Her cello playing slowed things down a bit because every hundred yards or so the good squire had to saw down a large tree to create a stump for her to sit on.

But all this laying out of streets, cello playing, and full-page ads in the *Globe* was to no avail. No one in Boston (Squire Granby's main target) was the least bit interested in a fifty-foot lot two hundred and thirty-two miles from the Copley Plaza. Try as he might, the squire could not hide the fact that there were no railroads, no highways, no steamship route to Granby View Acres. It was a real you-can't-get-there-from-here pollen-free resort area. In most ways it still is.

But Squire Granby was not a man who was easily defeated. He meditated for a long time and finally came up with a great idea—he'd *give* the land away! Granby View Acres needed people!

Boston still was not amused or impressed, and the first families (four) to take advantage of Squire Granby's offer were from Plymouth. They wanted to get away from that damn rock and its hordes of summer visitors.

These four families became the first settlers of Granby Lakes. They were the Turteltaubs, the Bloomballs, the Virgil Hoopleys, and Sarah Selby. Sam Turteltaub, the elder, was the first white man to step into a hidden ice hole in the lake and was never seen again. This was kind of an abrupt way to become regionally famous, but the family thought it was worthwhile in the end. A huge glacial boulder with a small bronze plaque was erected on the ice next to the ice hole, but it disappeared the first summer.

Miss Hinkley, Egil Grimshaw's emissary, was full of little anecdotes about the Granby Lakes area, which she recited like an LP recording, starting at the beginning again if any of us interrupted with a question. She was programmed for twaddle.

Miss Hinkley showed us eight or nine old homes situated on points and coves around the lake. Most of them had been built around the turn of the century and were greenly gray with terminal mildew. All of them had cavernous living rooms with a Citizen Kane fireplace crowned with the inevitable moosehead staring out at nothing. It seemed, as we progressed from one depressing lakeside home to another depressing lakeside home that the larger the moosehead the greater the price. All way out of our class.

I tested the toilets, as I had been instructed by a "How to buy a house" article in *Oui,* and not one of them ever flushed. The water in the bowls remained as placid as the pool in front of the Taj Mahal. Serenity, I felt, was not the quality one looks for in a flushed toilet bowl.

The parade of these lakeside (which was what we had wanted) enfeebled mansions that had obviously seen better days (at the time of the Crimean War) was just wasting our efforts.

"I think," Reiko said, "I go back to Japan"—which was what she always said when things got too much for her, and for once it sounded like a good idea. "I think I'll go with you," I said. "Me, too—me too," echoed our up-to-now quiet and patient children.

"Well," Miss Hinkley said sweetly, "I'm sure we'll find

something for you here in the lovely village of Granby Lakes—after all, Rome wasn't built in a day."

"I like Rome," I said. "Maybe we should look around there, maybe we'll—"

Miss Hinkley, I'm sure, could have bitten her tongue off at having mentioned Rome—or anywhere except Granby Lakes, but she smiled sweetly and said, "You wouldn't like Rome anymore—a lot of Italians moved in—loused up the whole neighborhood."

I studied Miss Hinkley quickly to see if she had suddenly become Groucho Marx, but she gave me her version of a Mona Lisa smile, which made her look like Harpo, and kept on driving.

As we moved through a small mountain pass, we saw it! A lovely gray building with high, steeply pitched roofs bookended with two massive chimneys, perched on top of a promontory overlooking, it seemed, all of Maine!

"Wow!" I said. "What the hell is *that!!!!???*"

CHAPTER

2

"WHAT the hell is that?" turned out to be The Old Sarah Selby Place which was now the Granby Lakes Hotel, and Miss Hinkley suggested subtly that the owners might want to sell.

"Not to us," Reiko said quickly. "We want a home—not a hotel."

"Yeah, we want a home, not a hotel," I said.

"I want a hotel," Timothy said.

"I want a hotel, too," Bobby said.

"I think it could be easily converted into a lovely home," Miss Hinkley said quickly. "It doesn't have to be a hotel—after all, it was once the Sarah Selby mansion."

"Just who," I asked, as Miss Hinkley practically goosed us through the front door, "was Sarah Selby?"

Miss Hinkley hesitated and then: "She was one of the first—people—ever to come to Granby Lakes—she built this place."

"She must have been loaded," Bobby said.

"Well," Miss Hinkley said, "she did very well—"

Mr. and Mrs. Tolland, the people who now owned the Sarah Selby place and ran it as a hotel, tried elaborately to appear not too eager to sell it. They were sitting in front of a fireplace that easily could have been converted to a two-car garage, plus plenty of room for a workshop for the man who likes to build cabin cruisers in fireplaces. They were playing a version of checkers. A version that I had read about in an old Graham Greene novel. They were playing with shot glasses filled with 180-proof vodka, and every time one would jump the other, they'd drink the captured vodka shot in one gulp. The board—in order to shorten the games—was laid out so that every move would be a triple jump.

Mr. Tolland, when he finally allowed himself to acknowledge that he had visitors, attempted to spring to his feet and bow graciously in imitation of the perfect host of the perfect inn. This sudden impulse to emulate Charles of the Ritz ended almost as quickly as it had begun. Mr. Tolland spilled his drink over his wife as his left knee caught the end of the coffee table and his right elbow sent a floor lamp crashing to the parquet. He recovered enough to shake Reiko's hand and say he was very pleased to know *me*. Mr. Tolland seemed to have a problem. We didn't know it then—but it was the Granby Lakes Hotel.

Miss Hinkley guided our tour of the old Sarah Selby Mansion-Granby Lakes Hotel, and once again we found ourselves in the vaulted living room. The Tollands, who had obviously completed several more games of Smirnoff checkers, attempted to stand up and bid us goodbye, which created another sorry, but kind of funny situation. The Tollands, Mark and Millie, only made it to their knees, giving the whole thing an aura of "An Afternoon with the Toulouse-Lautrecs."

"I love the place," I said, as soon as we were outside and could light a cigarette without fear of explosion.

"I knew you would," Miss Hinkley said, tears welling up in her large gray eyes.

21

"What's the matter?" Reiko wanted to know.

"Mommie, why is the lady crying?" Timothy said. I wanted to know, too. "Was it something I said?"

"No," Miss Hinkley said and kept on crying. Her false eyelashes became unglued and were carried downstream and just beneath her nose, making her look like any Greek actress before her morning shave.

"What the hell is it?" I said. Women's tears have long ago ceased to move me in any way except in the direction of unpremeditated homicide.

"It's just that"—Miss Hinkley was on the border of hysteria by this time—"it's just that I haven't sold anything since I've been working for Mr. Grimshaw, and I'm afraid."

"Afraid of Mr. Grimshaw?" Reiko said.

"What is he—some kind of a monster or something?" I said.

"No," Miss Hinkley sobbed. "He's the most kind and most sweet and—the nicest person I ever met. I just want to—to please him."

That kind of desire is highly commendable because it's so rare, but Reiko and I couldn't go around buying hotels just so the Miss Hinkleys of the world could happify the hearts of the Grimshaws of the world. We promised that we would be delighted (too strong a word) to come back the next day and further inspect the Granby Lakes Hotel.

The next day we got up to the Granby Lakes Hotel early. But not early enough. The Tollands had abandoned the time-consuming efforts of the checkerboard moves and confined themselves to the serious business of getting sloshed. Unimpeded. They were both on the verge of being unaware that they were not alone.

Millie Tolland, Mark Tolland's wife, was in a world of her own and could only have been reached through a medium.

Mark acknowledged our presence with a few well-chosen grunts.

"Mr. Tolland has had a bad cold," Miss Hinkley, the real estate woman, explained, then added quickly, "—which he caught on a trip down to Boston"—thus absolving Granby Lakes from any traffic in bad colds or any other bronchial disorders.

"Hardly anybody ever gets colds in Granby Lakes," she continued. "The air is so clean and pure."

"I thought colds came from germs," Reiko said. Reiko believed in honesty and direct answers.

Miss Hinkley took this in stride. "That may be true in Boston," she said, "but here in Granby Lakes there are *no germs!*"

"What do they do," I said, "sterilize you at the town line?"

"Mr. Douglas is a humorist," Miss Hinkley explained to the Tollands, which meant very little to them. Millie had by this time slumped forward and dropped most of her face into a deep-dish ashtray. Her breathing created periodic miniature tornados of Marlboro ash, swiftly covering everything with a soft gray coating which made everything look like the only color dogs can see.

"We'd better come back at another time," Miss Hinkley said.

"Yeah," Bobby, the always gracious almost teenager said, "they're drunk."

"Yes," Miss Hinkley said, "it's the Granby Lakes air—it's like wine."

"Jesus H. Buddha!" Bobby said. Bobby occasionally

bollixes up Eastern and Western dogmas (which may someday be the perfect solution).

On later visits that week to the Granby Lakes Hotel, Reiko and I and Bobby and Timothy tried to make up our minds whether to buy the place and spend the rest of our days admiring what I considered to be the absolute in lovely views. From the broad decks jutting from the front of the cocktail lounge, the dining room, and the mammoth kitchen, it seemed as if you could see forever. In reality, you could see the snow-capped peak of Mount Washington in New Hampshire seventy miles to the southwest. Just below was Granby Lake, a vast panorama of ever-changing blues and greens and silvers, beginning at the foot of Sugarback Mountain to the east and stretching far to the west, terminating in a low range of deep and dark purple hills, ridges, and mountains that marked the Canadian border.

On our last visit to what was rapidly becoming, to me, the most desirable piece of real estate I had ever had the good fortune to discover, I forgot completely that Miss Hinkley had set the casual trap just a few days before.

Our last visit also was coupled with a welcome surprise. Mark Tolland was on his feet, smiling and affable. Millie was nowhere to be seen. That didn't matter—we had Mark, and Mark was smilingly extolling the myriad advantages in owning this gold mine of a hotel.

"If it's such a gold mine," Reiko wanted to know, "why are you selling it?"

I wanted to know the answer to that, too, and so did Bobby. Timothy was interested in only one thing—where to put his sandbox?

"Well," Mark Tolland drawled; steadying himself by

gripping the deck railing, he continued, with great emphasis on insouciance and studied unconcern—"I have other interests, and the profit from this place puts me into a higher bracket. I just can't afford to make too much money." This didn't get through to Reiko at all. She never understood tax brackets, but I did. I understood Mr. Tolland's problem right away. And I sympathized with him, all the while secretly congratulating myself at having discovered this treasure trove.

Mr. Tolland was very helpful in pointing out the red-topped stakes that marked the boundaries of this golden opportunity. He also volunteered that everything was in perfect order. In all of the twenty-six motel and hotel units, there wasn't one single toilet that didn't flush! I was ecstatic! He also said that the septic tank had just been pumped out and was completely empty. Shangri-La!

Reiko asked about the heating system, which prompted Mr. Tolland to take us down into the very bowels of the hotel, where two Gargantuan furnaces stood side by side, like fat gladiators ready to fight off anything a vicious Maine winter might fling at the sturdy walls of the Granby Lakes Hotel. I had no idea whether the walls were sturdy or not, but I was assured that they were by Mr. Tolland: "eight inches wide and just jam-packed full of insulation—triple thickness."

Reiko asked Mr. Tolland to start up the furnaces so she would know how to turn them on. Mr. Tolland said he would be more than glad to start the furnaces going full blast, but unfortunately, Mr. Beardsley, their caretaker, was down to Rumford having a tooth pulled, and he was the only one who knew how to turn on the furnaces. Mr. Tolland evidently was more like the captain of a ship. He just gave the orders. He didn't do any of the dirty work himself.

I asked Mr. Tolland about the taxes, but unfortunately Mr. Hoopley, who took care of things like that, was down to Farmington visiting his ailing mother and wouldn't be back for a while.

The man who took care of the plumbing had gone to Portland to buy his wife something nice for their anniversary and unfortunately wasn't available for any inquiry about the sprinkling system (there was a sprinkler head in every room). Poor Mr. Tolland, he had no idea how it worked—he had just spent ten thousand dollars having it installed and he felt that he had done enough. He wasn't interested in the technical side of things. Just so long as they did the job.

We asked to see the books, but the accountant who took care of the books was in Hawaii on a vacation and had presumably taken the books with him—for safe-keeping.

The guest list, showing previous customers of the Granby Lakes Hotel, must have been a prodigious one—based on the hotel's remarkable longevity, it having first opened its doors as a hotel on July 17, 1908. Mr. Tolland assured me that I was quite correct in assuming that they *did* have a lengthy guest list, but at the moment it was unavailable because they had sent it to a bindery in Boston to be bound into fabulous old Moroccan leather covers, embossed, of course, with gold lettering. All that takes time, Mr. Tolland continued, but the bound guest list (twenty-five volumes) "should be back any day now."

There were so many things we asked about because,

for the kind of money Mr. Tolland was asking for this lovely hostelry, we wanted to make sure that everything was just exactly as Mark Tolland *assured us* it *was. Over* and *over.* We were too dewy-eyed to notice the zealous repetition.

"I like Mr. Tolland," Reiko said when we had a moment alone. "He's so honest and aboveboard about everything—like—about the roof."

"Yeah," I agreed, "he didn't have to tell us that the roof was guaranteed for twenty years, and there's only ten years left on the guarantee."

"What company did he say put the roof on?"

"He didn't say."

"And you can make a lot of money in the bar from the people who play golf," Tolland advised us just as we were leaving.

"Golf?" I said. "There's a golf course near here?"

"Of course!" Tolland was astonished. "Right across the way—"

"I thought those were just nice green hills."

"They are, but they're kept nice and green by a crew of maintenance men." Tolland took us out to the front entrance of the hotel and, with a broad sweep, showed us the golf course, and sure enough that's what it was. With gay red flags poking up from every immaculate green.

"Where are the golfers?" Reiko said, practically.

"You'll love Mr. Yates," Tolland continued.

"Who?"

"Thomas E. Yates, the owner of the golf course—he comes from your neck of the woods—Connecticut—he's a prince of a fellow."

"Well," I said, "I don't really remember meeting any

27

princes of fellows in Connecticut—not that there couldn't be a few around."

Tolland laughed. "Well," he said, "you'll meet one soon, and there isn't anything he wouldn't do to—" Tolland didn't finish this.

"Where are the golfers?" Reiko insisted.

"Oh," Mark Tolland said, "today is Saturday—not many golfers play golf on Saturday."

"Funny," I said, "I thought that Saturday was the big day—for golfers."

"Just look at that ninth green, almost right at your front door," Tolland went on, blithely, I think is the right word. And "purposely oblivious" would be two more right words.

"Gee, Papa—that's great—we'll be getting a lot of golf balls right in our living room!" was Bobby's contribution.

"What?" Reiko said

"I understand," Tolland said, posthaste (another right word), "that they are going to move the ninth green next week and put it on the other side of the eighth green—*way* over *there!*" He pointed at the Canadian border or maybe just a little beyond it.

CHAPTER

3

THERE'S no way I can get around admitting that Reiko and I bought the Granby Lakes Hotel, but I must qualify that—we bought it for a residence. A home. At the first opportunity we intended to sell off two motel buildings (five units each) and two small cottages. Everything was to be moved away from the lovely main building which we would use as a home.

The "closing" is a legal ceremony, during which you sign many, many mysterious papers and the buyer and the seller smile at each other—for the last time.

The closing was held in the real estate office of Grimshaw and Poseidon. Egil Grimshaw, who was also a lawyer (and was also Poseidon) would represent Mark and Millie Tolland, the seller. Reiko and I had arrived early and were greeted by Egil Grimshaw who was extremely happy to meet us and, to put us at ease, assured us warmly that he was "just plain folks," as he sat there in his high-backed desk chair and snapped his baby-blue suspenders against his red-checkered shirt—which was more than well-buttoned by six three-carat diamond buttons. A bright yellow necktie flowed down and over a paunch that looked like an inflated safety airbag for a new Sherman tank. Here was a man who lived well. His frontal enormity was accented by a diamond horseshoe in his necktie that would have fit a Clydesdale. His cuff links were designed like cute miniature traffic signals, made from an emerald, a topaz, and a ruby.

"Do they light up?" I asked. He smiled and waved his hands like Nixon used to do toward the end of his reign. Mr. Grimshaw was also featuring an opal-studded wedding ring on his left hand, which covered two fingers. His right hand was festooned with a collection of star sapphires—one on each finger and each bigger than the other. Sammy Davis would have killed himself.

In deference to good taste, Egil Grimshaw's right thumb was unadorned. I suppose that's what he meant when he said he was "just plain folks."

"I've seen you people on the TV many times," Egil Grimshaw said, I suppose to make us feel right at home in Granby Lakes. "I loved you on *Marcus Welby, M.D.*"— needless to say—a talk show we have never been on.

"Thank you," we said.

Egil Grimshaw's office where much of the action took place at first was unbelievable to anybody who could read. Instead of wallpaper he had law degrees. If he had graduated from each of these law schools, he must have been a student for one hundred and twenty-seven years.

"You go to all these law schools?" I asked.

"Yeah," Egil said. "Of course—some of them are honorary. Did you know I was the state's attorney here for a number of years?"

I knew it now. "How about this one here," I asked, indicating something that looked like a badly neglected Dead Sea Scroll.

"Oh yes," Egil said, "that one. There's an amusing

story that goes with that one." I waited, but he didn't amuse me with the story.

"I'll bet there's an amusing story that goes with this one," I said, pointing to another framed document.

"Oh, yes." Egil beamed his warmest. I waited, but it was a fruitless pause, no amusing story came forth.

I thought I'd give it one more try. I pointed to a law degree from Clemson. "Clemson?" I said.

"Oh, yes," Egil said, "charming place—North Carolina."

"South Carolina," I said, because I knew where it was.

"Naturally," Egil Grimshaw said, his eyes narrowing into a smiling lynx expression. Right then and there I decided that here was a man who would never be trapped—because he never said anything. That is, he never said anything that couldn't be interpreted in eight different ways, all of them devious but noncommittal, and loaded with two-way guile.

We learned more about Egil Grimshaw after we lived in Granby Lakes for a while. He was a multimillionaire. He also owned the Granby Lakes bank, but this never prevented him from being "just plain folks" with any-one, and especially with some comely widow he was about to have his bank evict from the family farm be-cause last year's potato crop had failed. In this icy-cold part of Maine the potato crop fails every year, but some years it fails worse than others, and those times are called eviction times in Egil Grimshaw's book. If the widow was comely enough, Egil Grimshaw would hint that a little copula profundis might stall the eviction no-tice, but if his bulling in her china shop was not entirely sexually satisfactory to Egil Grimshaw and his acrobatic performance in the back seat of his Cadillac convertible,

31

the eviction notice would be handed to the comely widow as she was dropped off at the family farm (her shredded long johns in her purse).

Our lawyer was Joseph F. Fulman, who had been highly recommended over the telephone by Mrs. Thomas E. Yates, the wife of the Connecticut prince of a fellow, who owned the golf course right across the way from the hotel which was now almost within our deliriously happy grasp.

Joseph F. Fulman looked like an unreliable 747 pilot, and apparently anyone who respected Joseph F. Fulman as a lawyer would be considered in Granby Lakes as slightly retarded. Nevertheless, our Mrs. Thomas E. Yates' highly recommended lawyer suddenly became very busy, after the "closing" got under way, making sure that we signed as many papers as possible. After we had scribbled our names and initials on everything but each other's genitals, we all sat back and relaxed with a cup of instant coffee. We weren't too far into this phase of the closing when Joseph F. Fulman said to me, "You got a piece of property you didn't expect to get, eh?"

"I beg your pardon?"

"I said—you got a piece of land you didn't expect to get—"

"For Chrissakes! You mean we signed the wrong papers!"

"No, no, no," Joseph F. Fulman said in a tone that was pure treacle. "I mean this piece of property here—" He produced a map by conjuration and pointed to the northeast corner.

"This twenty-five-foot strip is now yours."

"Gee, that's very nice of you," Reiko said.

"Very nice of Mr. Tolland," Joseph F. Fulman said.

Mr. Tolland, the former owner, was not present at the closing, which I thought was strange, but he had signed all the documents beforehand, so maybe it didn't really matter.

"Yeah," I said, not at all interested in a twenty-five-foot strip of land that bordered the opposite side of the road. "That Mr. Tolland is another prince of a fellow."

"And this little twenty-five-foot strip you're losing down here doesn't mean a thing anyway," Joseph F. Fulman soothed, adding more treacle and a quarter of a pound of melted butter.

"What?" I said. "What 'little strip' we're *losing?*"

"This little strip down here in the southwest corner—doesn't mean a thing."

Egil Grimshaw, representing the absent Mr. Tolland, suddenly came to life. "Yeah, Jack, that little twenty-five-foot strip down in the southwest corner doesn't go with your property—it was sold—oh—long ago."

Nobody else said anything while Reiko and I looked at each other, then at Joseph F. Fulman, Egil Grimshaw, Egil Grimshaw's secretary, Miss Hinkley, and Egil Grimshaw's partner, who was represented by an empty chair—this was Mr. Poseidon, who was also Mr. Grimshaw. Miss Hinkley started to cry.

"Doesn't mean a thing," Egil Grimshaw said again, sliding a box of reinforced Kleenex over to Miss Hinkley.

"If it doesn't mean anything," I innocently put forth, "why would anybody buy it? What the hell good is a twenty-five-foot strip of land? Somebody got big ideas about putting in a string of 'mobile homes'?" The very euphemism "mobile home" bruised my artistic sensitivity; they were, so far as I was concerned, nothing more than highly painted, gussied-up versions of the shanties that used to line the Santa Fe tracks every few miles and housed the Chicanos who sweated out their days keeping the right-of-way in shape for the Super Chief. Mobile home was another name for ghetto in my tear-stained book, and I visualized a row of them up and down that twenty-five-foot strip we had just lost.

"You don't understand, Jack," Joseph F. Fulman started before I cut him off.

"All I understand is—we have been negotiating for months and months for this hotel and the land upon which it stands and the grounds which surround it—and the grounds which surround it include that twenty-five-foot strip! In the southwest corner!" Egil Grimshaw hastily grabbed up all the signed papers on the cigarette-butt-marked conference table and shoved them into his attaché case—which promptly swallowed them. Egil Grimshaw expected trouble, but he didn't get it. Not then anyway.

"But, Jack, that twenty-five-foot strip was sold months ago," Joseph F. Fulman insisted again, as though repetition would smooth the way to reasonableness. It makes me laugh now—bitterly perhaps or, more correctly, cynically—because we found out a few months later that the twenty-five-foot strip in question had been sold on the *same day* we were sitting in Egil Grimshaw's office closing our deal for the hotel. The strip had been sold to a man in Massachusetts and the man in Massachusetts had been represented by—Joseph F. Fulman.

The ignominious news concerning the twenty-five-foot strip prompted me to bring up a question I had brought up many times before. Monotonously, tediously, and tenaciously.

"What does that little paragraph I have never been able to get an answer to mean? 'Excepting and reserving those interests and rights accorded Thomas E. Yates, *et al.*' Thomas E. Yates, the golf course owner, has reserved interests and rights in a piece of property which we have just paid a fabulous price for—what the hell does that mean? I wanna know *right now!*" My tone almost caused a stampede. Egil Grimshaw clutched his briefcase; Miss Hinkley dropped her glasses and covered her imaginary tits, while Joseph F. Fulman just raised his brows in amazement at my righteous indignation, then smoothly explained that Thomas E. Yates' interests and rights meant simply that if he knocked a golf ball onto our property, he and *et al.* would have a right to come onto our property and pick it up.

"Who's *et al.?*" Reiko asked.

"That's Latin," Joseph F. Fulman, who was rapidly becoming Wylie's bride at every funeral and corpse at every wedding, explained.

"For Chrissakes!" I yelled. "Stop being evasive for Chrissakes! Tell her what it means!" I was tired and hot and fed up with this legal chameleon.

"Oh," Joseph F. Fulman said, momentarily shedding his Mr. Hyde skin, "it means 'And others'—you know, a few others—like his wife and maybe a few friends."

When we hired this paragon of nonvirtue, we had asked him what he was going to charge us.

"Don't worry about it," Joseph F. Fulman said. But I did worry about it, and I asked him many times what the legal fees were going to be for this simple transaction. (All a lawyer does is go to the county courthouse and flip through a few abstracts of title—a job that would take fifteen minutes if he dawdled.) And the fee is still exorbitant, but I suppose we must take into consideration that lawyers *do* study and *do* have to memorize a certain amount of legal *mumbo* and *jumbo* with which to confuse us mortal clods.

The day after the closing Joseph F. Fulman's bill was delivered by a special messenger (presumably traveling by rocket). The bill knocked me down three times (I counted).

He had included everything, even the ten cents he had been forced to cough up in order to use a pay toilet at Grant's City. In downtown Wilton. What Grant's City in Wilton, Maine, had in common with our title-search was never really fully explained. Maybe, I thought, our newly acquired property and the land upon which Grant's City rested was once part of a huge plantation, given by King George III to one of his psychiatrists (most likely to the one who told him he was sane), and Joseph F. Fulman had to check it out—to make sure our boundaries didn't conflict with W. T. Grant's pizza counter, although we were some sixty-five miles up-country from there—or maybe Joseph F. Fulman was trying to pad his bill by ten cents. Other items on his overitemized bunco sheet were "Travel Expenses $136.02 at 38 cents per mile." I questioned this, as I did almost everything on his bill except the ten cents for his side trip to Grant's Toiletland. That was *our* treat.

There really was no explanation for Joseph F. Fulman's travel expenses because his web was right across the street from the county courthouse, where the fifteen-minute title-search would have taken place, that is, if he title-searched at all.

Something else that Reiko and I could not understand was an item listed as "phone calls, $110.35." When

36

I asked Joseph F. Fulman whom he had called, he said, "My dear boy, a lawyer has to make phone calls to many people—how could I possibly remember whom I called?"

Reiko thought it was about time to do a little cross-examination. "If you don't remember whom you called, how did you arrive at one hundred ten dollars and thirty-five cents? Do you have an itemized list?"

"No, I don't have an itemized list!" Joseph F. Fulman was steadily becoming more incensed at our impertinent inquiries. "And if I did, you would not be allowed to see it! My records are confidential!"

"Well in that case," I said, "I'm a little confidential myself, but I'll tell *you*."

"Tell me what?" Joseph F. Fulman was cautious.

"Can you keep a confidential secret?"

"What—confidential secret?"

"I'm not going to pay your bill."

Joseph F. Fulman, to give him the best of it, kept his cool, but he said, as he was leaving, "If that's the way you feel, okay—but I'm gonna fix you."

Before he got a chance to fix us—Joseph F. Fulman was indicted by the U.S. grand jury—on nine counts —of fixing somebody else.

Maybe, as dear Joey Gallo said just before he got his head blown off in Umberto's Clam House, "Retribution is one of the grand principles in the divine administration of human affairs; a requital is imperceptible only to the willfully unobservant. There is everywhere the working of the everlasting law of requital: Man always gets as he gives."

(Actually, for the record, dear Joey didn't get to say quite *all* of this.)

CHAPTER

4

"HEY, mister, you wanna buy some Girl Scout cookies?" This came from a darling little green-eyed pixie of a girl. She had the face of a double-dealing angel. She also had beautiful blond silky hair pulled tight with a large green ribbon. Her hands were filthy, and she held out an opened box of Girl Scout cookies which must have been baked two years before. Some of them were gray and some of them were darker gray. This happened after the ordeal. "Ordeal" and "closing" are interchangeable words.

Reiko and I and our two, by this time, snarling children were sitting in The Yellow Apple, a Granby Lakes eatery, famous for its stomach-pump therapy.

"Mr. Couzy says you are going to buy the Granby Lakes Hotel, you wanna buy some Girl Scout cookies?"

"We just bought the Granby Lakes Hotel, and I don't want to buy any Girl Scout cookies," I said. This did not turn the cookie seller off.

"Mr. Couzy says he figured you for a dum-dum."

"Wait a minute," I said, between sips of one of The Yellow Apple's specialties—poisoned coffee with cream that was about to turn. "Who are you? Or maybe, first, who is Mr. Couzy?"

"He's the one who said he figured you for a dum-dum."

"I know," I said in my best let's-be-kind-to-the-Iguanas manner. "But who is this Couzy fellow who figured me for a dum-dum?"

"He's my father—he's the Granby Lakes' barber—my name is Betsy Couzy, you wanna buy some Girl Scout cookies and maybe hear a little more?" I bought the ancient Girl Scout cookies, and the darling little green-eyed Betsy Couzy curtsied like little girls used to curtsy to their elders back around the turn of the century when little girls grew up and became ladies instead of Rex Reed. It was quite refreshing.

"I think we'd better go," Reiko said. "What'll I do with these cookies?"

"Bury them," Bobby said.

"I wanna cookie," Timothy said, his mouth filled to overflowing with a blend of half hamburger and half ketchup. The ketchup was also a large part of his chin decor.

"No," Reiko said, "you'll spoil your dinner. Come on. Let's go."

"Wait," I said, "I want to hear more." Then I said to Betsy Couzy, "What else were you going to tell me?"

"Well," Betsy Couzy said, "for one thing—Roger Quakenbush has been humping Bella Bagby, up behind the old mill. If you wanna hear more, you'll have to buy more cookies—"

"Quick, Papa, buy some more cookies!" Bobby said. Bobby was at the age when he wanted to augment his ignorance with something other than just Sesame Street and The Electric Theater and Zoom.

39

"Betsy," I said, "nice little girls don't go around saying things like that."

"Like what?" Betsy said, her eyes all wide and innocent like Doris Day's—used to be.

"Like what you said about Roger what's-his-name and Bella Bagby. Supposing Bella Bagby heard this, then what?"

"Jeeeez," Betsy Couzy said, "what's the big secret? She was the first to know!" I could see that I wasn't getting through to this down-east Rona Barrett, so I tried to channel things in a different direction.

"How do you like living in Granby Lakes?" I said. "It certainly must be a wonderful place for little girls and boys to grow up in."

"Yeah," Betsy agreed. "Wow! Are they gonna sock it to *you!*"

"What's that mean?" Reiko wanted to know. (They didn't use phrases like "sock it to you" in Japan except when you're buying a used Honda.)

"They sock it to everybody who buys that old dump of a Granby Lakes Hotel—that's what my father says."

"Why would they do that?"

"Because ever since the mill closed back in 1923, the Granby Lakes Hotel is the only successful business in town—but only if it flops. The Granby Lakes Hotel has been bankrupt, foreclosed, and repossessed or whatever forty-nine times since 1923. The pipes and the toilets have been frozen solid every winter since 1923. The title to the property has been in dispute since 1923, and the liens against the hotel are uncountable—and the final score still isn't in—"

"But we had a title search done by—"

Betsy Couzy continued, happily, "Nobody's done a ti-

40

tle search on that place since 1924. They don't have to bother—they know it'll go under before they go back—even two owners ago."

"I don't understand this," Reiko said.

"I wanna cookie," Timothy said.

"Shut up," Bobby said.

"Wait a minute," I said. "Betsy—that your name? You puzzle me. How could a hotel failure benefit *anybody?* Besides we're not going to run the place as a hotel—we're going to use it as a home, a private residence. We're going to sell the motels and the cottages—"

"My God!" Betsy said. "They got you on that one, too! Wow! My father's right about you—you *are* a dumdum."

"You mean—nobody will buy the motels and cottages and move them out of there?"

"Sure they'll buy 'em, but Mr. Grimshaw's bank won't let you sell 'em!" This revelation really turned Betsy Couzy on—she was beaming.

"You mean," Reiko said, "we'll have to keep it as a hotel-motel—and run it like that?"

"You can try!" Betsy said.

"Why," I said, all the ecstasy and joy of owning a place in this beautiful section of the world temporarily gone, "why are you telling us this?"

"Because," Betsy Couzy said, "there's nothing else for little girls to do here in Granby Lakes, other little girls skip rope or play jacks or steal grapes. That kind of stuff doesn't appeal to me, so I just go around selling Girl Scout cookies and telling everybody everything I know—I'm a squealer."

"An informer," Bobby said.

"I like that better," Betsy Couzy said, smiling at Bobby. "I'm an informer. So if you wanna know something—and would like to buy some Girl Scout cookies—"

"Maybe you'd better go outside and play," I suggested. I wanted to think about what I had just heard.

"You mean—play 'doctor'?"

"That's an idea," I said.

"But not with Roger Quakenbush—right?"

"Who's Roger Quakenbush?" I'd forgotten.

"He's the one who's been humping Bella—"

"Never mind!"

"—Bagby. If you need any Girl Scout cookies, I'm in the book. 'Bye!"

Betsy Couzy ran out the door, but not before she snatched the box of cookies she had just sold me.

CHAPTER

5

DURING the eight-hour drive back to Connecticut, Reiko and I discussed—as much as we could between the violent sibling wars taking place in the backseat (which seemed never-ending between Bobby and Timothy)—the recent events in Maine.

"It might be fun—running a hotel," Reiko said. "They have a lovely cocktail lounge. I could be the bartender, and you could entertain."

"I've entertained for the last time," I said. "In cocktail lounges—too many drunks—they never listen to my jokes."

"In your own cocktail lounge you wouldn't have to put up with that," Reiko said. "If someone annoyed you, you could throw them out."

"I couldn't throw out Twiggy," I said.

"I wonder why that little girl said that the people in Granby Lakes Village only did good when the hotel flopped?"

"I guess she meant that the bank would make money—selling it again. The real estate man—he'd make money from a resale, and all the local carpenters, plumbers, etc., would make money fixing things up for the new owner."

"You mean—things fall apart between owners?"

43

"I would say that's a safe bet—and probably during the time the new owner is trying to make a go of it. Especially if the new owner was a little on the dumb side. At least *we* know, from our two years in Canada—fixing things for ourselves—what to do during some emergency—like a stuck bathroom or something. I don't think they'll be able to fool us—"

"Yeah," Reiko agreed. "But what about *twenty-six* stuck bathrooms?"

When we arrived in Connecticut, we couldn't wait to tell our friends and neighbors in Honansville all about our grandiose acquisition and the great promise of our life in one of the most sensationally attractive areas of our beloved country.

"Don't move to *Maine!*" was the advice we got from all sides.

Henry Rosemont, our accountant and business manager: "They'll break your balls!" Mr. Rosemont was at his most flowery when it came to expressing himself about the human race.

"How?" I yelled over the phone, galled by the fact that the person I most trusted and probably had the most respect for—because of his brilliant handling of my finances—had the audacity to disagree with me.

"First," Henry Rosemont said, "they'll con you into something—*anything.* They are the greatest con men in the world—those people. In Connecticut, you can spot a con man—in Maine, you'll never know until you've been skewered."

"I can take care of myself," I said. It was almost a question. "I know what I'm doing." Another almost question.

"Sure you do," Henry Rosemont too readily agreed. "Remember that Vassar girl you met in a bar in Las Vegas—her mother needed an operation?" This had happened in my carefree bachelor days when I was a drummer in a band.

"What about it?"

"You paid for the operation—three hundred and fifty dollars—and what did you get out of it?"

"I got the satisfaction of helping someone who was in trouble—*that's* what I got out of it!" I was hurt by the implication that I'd expected to *get* something from this lovely girl with the magnificent bosoms. Ridiculous!

There was a small pause. "Jack," Henry said, "*you* are a *mark!*"

"That was a long time ago," I said, "and who the hell cares. I'm smarter now, and anyway we bought this hotel and we're going to move up there!" There was a long ominous pause after this. "Henry, are you still there?"

"You"—another ominous pause—"you bought a *hotel?* A hotel in Maine!!!"

"Yes," I said, "in a resort area—you know, hunting, fishing, boating, snowmobiling, skiing, swimming."

"Swimming! In *Maine!?*"

"Sure," I said, "they swim up there!"

"You don't mean people, I hope—you mean salmon, right?"

"No, people." I wasn't so sure now. "Don't people swim in Maine?"

"Once," he said, "just once. Jack, let me tell you about one of my friends who bought a hotel up there."

"Did they break his balls?"

"Not only that. He lost his ass, his hotel, his wife, his AT&T stock, his Cadillac, his station wagon, and his marbles—he's now locked up in a rubber room in Bangor. He was one of my biggest clients until he bought the Granby Lakes Hotel."

CHAPTER

6

MR. Titterford was a jolly fat man who owned the Titterford Hill Dairy "down-country" from the Granby Lakes area. Mr. Titterford was jolly and fat—only in his jolly fat man ads, which he featured in the Granby Lakes *Daily News,* which had never been "daily" in its entire publishing life. The Granby Lakes *Daily News* appeared once a month at best, and once every two months, which was better yet. But Mr. Titterford's full-page advertisements appeared whenever the paper did, and they pictured Mr. Titterford laughing uproariously at something (probably the price of milk) and saying in a balloon above his sparse head (his hair wasn't sparse—his head was) things like: "Titterford's milk is like the kind Mother used to make only ours is Pasteurized!" Which, of course, made it sound like mothers had better boil their knockers if they wanted to be really with it.

Our experience with Mr. Titterford had to do with his sudden appearance in the kitchen of our hotel on the day we moved in.

 ."Are you folks gonna use Titterford's Grade A Pasteurized milk or not?" Mr. Titterford said, without a trace of jollity. In fact, I thought his manner was more like a loan shark speaking with a victim who was one payment behind.

"How did you get into our kitchen?" I parried, not too brightly, but I wanted to know because we always kept the front door locked, a habit we had picked up back in civilization. "How did you get in the front door?"

"I have a key," Mr. Titterford said.

Reiko and I looked at each other, then at Mr. Titterford. "You have a key?" we both said.

"Yeah," Mr. Titterford said, not blinking. I was sure his eyelids closed up—from the bottom—like any other reptile's.

"Why?" I said.

"Look," Mr. Titterford said, "I'm Mr. Titterford."

"Oh," I said.

"Who's Mr. Titterford?" Reiko rightfully wanted to know.

"*He* is," I explained, equally as rightfully.

"You see, m'am," Mr. Titterford, softened a little bit, "if I didn't have no key and you wasn't to home, I couldn't get in."

"But," Reiko said, "we're always—to home."

"Well, maybe so," Mr. Titterford gracefully acknowledged, "but some of the other forty-nine folks who owned this here hotel wasn't to home when I called, and that way I couldn't get rid of no milk. *No how.*"

I wanted to ask Mr. Titterford if he had majored in English, but something kept telling me that it would only start trouble if I did.

Mr. Titterford took out a little milk-stained notebook, and a pencil which he chewed into a point, then he spread his legs, planted his feet deep down into the linoleum of the kitchen floor, and said, "How many gallons of Titterford's milk you folks gonna want a day?"

47

It was then that I realized that this unjolly fat man may have been what Little Betsy Couzy meant when she said they would sock it to us. This, I felt, might be a preview of the new off-TV season which was coming up.

Before I could warn her, Reiko said, "How many gallons do we have to take?"

"Oh, about—" Mr. Titterford started making scratch marks in his little Book of Days.

"Wait a minute," I said. "We don't want any milk at all."

Mr. Titterford couldn't believe what he had just heard. It was like a galley slave refusing to man his oar when Telly Savalas suggested he do so—punctuating his suggestion with a few meaningful slashes across the galley slave's back with a nail-studded cat-o'nine-tails.

"You—"—Mr. Titterford was enunciating now— "don't—want—ANY—milk?"

His tone upset me. I looked for his nail-studded cat-o'-nine-tails, but all I saw was his little black book and his little chewed pencil. It's a gas gun, I thought. His little chewed pencil is a gas gun! I almost said it out loud.

Mr. Titterford moved deliberately now. First, he snapped the cover of his little black book shut, with a meaningful "thunk"—then he shoved his little chewed pencil into its special niche in his upper breast pocket. Patted the pocket to make sure it was there, then he turned and "seized"—that was the only word I could think of—he seized our hundred-gallon stainless steel and brass seven-hundred-and-fifty-dollar milk dispenser from its honored place in our spotless kitchen and strode toward the door with it. He was, at that moment, an irresistible force—with the unlikelihood of ever meeting up with an immovable object. I couldn't help myself—I found I was opening doors for this juggernaut. Maybe I was protecting the doors from being splintered into future kindling. I don't know why I did it.

Mr. Titterford steamed through the front doorway and out to the open tailgate of his pickup truck. Here, with a mighty farting heave, he deposited our priceless (now) milk dispenser onto the tailgate and shoved it into the back end of the truck. Then again, all insulting deliberation, he slammed the tailgate shut and spike-locked it into place.

Suddenly, anger welled up inside me, anger and a little stupidity, considering that Mr. Titterford was six foot four and weighed two hundred and fifty pounds and had hands like two steel wrecking balls.

"Wait a minute!" I screamed, my voice cracking a little as *I* tried to sound like *he* looked. "What the hell do you think you're doing?" As I said this, I stepped toward him, just enough to be three inches outside of the reach of his two steel wrecking balls.

"I'm taking my milk dispenser—somewhere—where it will be appreciated."

"But that's our milk dispenser!" Reiko said. "We paid for it—we got an inventory."

"I don't care what you got, lady. It's my milk dispenser and I'm takin' it!"

And that's exactly what he did.

Two minutes after Mr. Titterford drove with screeching tires down our driveway and out of our lives, I was on the phone to the county attorney. He said he'd see what he could do about Mr. Titterford and our milk dispenser. I never found out what he did, but after a month or so we got a note from him saying that Mr. Titterford had done nothing illegal. The county attorney also enclosed an affidavit from Mr. Titterford. The affidavit said nothing about us or our particular milk dispenser. It just said that Mr. Titterford had sworn that he had done nothing illegal. This, so far as we were concerned, was like the San Francisco earthquake stating that San Francisco had shoved *first*.

At the time, we had no way of knowing that this was to be the pattern for a long list of seizures—by claimants who had nothing more than their word and a lot of down east chutzpah. They also had a gift of timing. It always happened when we were not in the hotel. It didn't matter if we were gone for fifteen minutes to pick up the mail at the Granby Lakes P.O. or that we were on an all-day excursion "down-country" to the nearest Western Auto Store to replace a few of the items which had been liberated by our Granby Lakes' fan club.

"How do they get in?" Reiko kept asking me, and I kept telling her that everybody seemed to have a key. Changing the locks did no good. Everybody still had a key, which apparently had been furnished by Earl Harkins, the Granby Lakes' locksmith. Earl Harkins was also the Granby Lakes' drunk and school bus driver. Legend has it that he became a locksmith because every time he got drunk he locked himself out of the school bus, and Tydings Humpley, who was the assistant village drunk, suggested that if Earl Harkins would like to keep his school bus driving job he'd better learn how to pick a lock. And that's just what Earl Harkins did. And supplemented his drinking fund quite substantially because he was the only locksmith in Granby Lakes. Not that there was much call for a locksmith in Granby

Lakes because as everybody in Granby Lakes is very fond of saying, "We never lock our doors"—which sounds real friendly-like, but it may be the reason so many people miss a lot of little things like refrigerators and stoves and sometimes even wives. (The wives, usually, were returned.)

One of the items claimed by a Mr. Porter was our lawn mower. He told us that he had lent this particular lawn mower to a Mr. Clyde Spraling some years before. And Mr. Spraling had never returned it. Reiko and I felt that this lawn mower wasn't really worth fighting about—at the moment—that came later when a Mr. Updike came by and offered to sell us a lawn mower.

Mr. Updike had cleaned the lawn mower, so it looked brand-new. Also he had cleaned it so well we saw the name GRANBY LAKES HOTEL etched in the metal of one of the cutting blades. I quickly grabbed the lawn mower and slammed the door in Mr. Updike's face. Mr. Updike left after that, but before he did he wrote something on the front door (we could hear the scratching). When Mr. Updike was out of sight, we opened the door cautiously, in case of ambush, and saw what Mr. Updike had written on our front door. It was not a word—it was a hex sign. The worst kind of hex sign—especially for the Granby Lakes Hotel—the hex sign meant "Good Luck." Days after Mr. Updike had left, we smelled sulfur, and we found later he belonged to a very esoteric sect. He was a Polish Druid.

Nevertheless, I now felt that I was part of the Granby Lakes' "family," which, it didn't take me long to realize, gave me about as much power and prestige as a Jewish dwarf, with a speech impediment, would have as a member of a Mafia "family" in Naples.

51

CHAPTER

7

WAY back in 1752, before Ben Franklin became our ambassador and started to fool around with girls in Paris, he was nothing, and messing with kites in Philadelphia. But only during thunderstorms. One particularly loud day he got knocked flat by a large jolt of lightning. And that told him something he didn't forget: "Never fly a kite during a thunderstorm in Philadelphia." He later used it as a filler line in his *Poor Richard's Almanac*. (There was some space left at the bottom of page 86, right after "Early to bed, early to rise," and other bad advice.)

But flying a kite in a thunderstorm in Philadelphia pushed electricity into the big time. Before Ben had had his eyebrows singed off by a bolt, no one had given this powerful force a second thought. They didn't know that, with electricity going for you, you could burn up all the oil on earth in a much shorter time than without it. You could also run a washing machine, a dryer, a toothbrush, a vacuum cleaner, an air-conditioner, a power saw, a can opener, a toaster, Pizza signs, and so many, many other essentials, including the Louisa May Alcott vibrator, which was mentioned in *The Reader's Digest* series, "I Am Joe's Dildoe."

Electricity for the Granby Lakes area was furnished

by the Granby Lakes Power Company, at the highest rate per KWH in the world. And why not? It's the only game in town.

The Granby Lakes Power Company was founded by Aldous McGill, a canny Scotsman, and was immediately swallowed up by the political machinations of one Richard N. Huckle. Maybe Aldous wasn't too canny because in no time at all he was demoted from president and chairman of the board of the Granby Lakes Power Company to an assistant meter reader.

Richard N. Huckle was an ambitious wheeler and dealer. He was also a member of the National Rifle Association and could shoot the eye out of a fly at fifty yards, which is one reason you see so many flies with eye patches in Maine. Tydings Herley, the assistant village drunk, told everybody.

Richard N. Huckle had frightened Aldous McGill into selling him all his stock in the Granby Lakes Power Company merely by hinting that he knew something evil about Aldous McGill's past—which was ridiculous because Aldous McGill had never done a wrong thing *ever* in his life. He hadn't even wet his pants when he was a baby. He held it until he was big enough to stand up to the bowl all by himself—and then he let go. *The Guinness Book of World Records* records it as a record: Aldous McGill passed water twenty-four hours a day for almost two years. And if you can't believe Mr. Guinness, who the hell can you believe?

But to continue with *As the World Turns*—Richard N. Huckle's political machinations did not stop at the acquisition of the Granby Lakes Power Company. From what I've heard about him, his impossible dream was to take over the entire state, so he ran for office and won.

53

His first political title was "Inspector of Roads"—a job he did very well. In fact, he did it all his *first day* in office. He got a large map of Maine which was crisscrossed with highways, and he pointed to each one, in front of his secretary, who was also a notary public, and said, "*This* is a road. *This* is a road. *That* is a road—" He kept this up until he had pointed at every road in the state. This act was duly witnessed and notarized by his secretary, and Richard N. Huckle took off on a three-hundred-sixty-four-day vacation.

The next time he ran for office was when old Mr. Putney died and Furbish County needed a new representative right away. Richard N. Huckle plowed under his only rival for the job—*Mrs.* Putney—by spreading the rumor that she and Mr. Putney had never been married—and you *know* what that made their thirteen children and eighty-four grandchildren! The referendum voters in Furbish County never bothered to check out this rumor; it was a helluva lot more fun to believe it to be true. That's how Richard N. Huckle stepped his second step up the political ladder—on rungs and rungs of bastards.

Richard N. Huckle wasn't too happy about being just a representative at the statehouse in the capital—because he was just one of hundreds of representatives, a position Richard N. Huckle found unbearable. He wanted to be one of a kind on the political scene. This was an understandable, if at that moment, an implausible ambition. They weren't quite ready to make him governor. And the governor wasn't quite ready to step down and make way for this pushy upstart, even though Richard N. Huckle had hinted that he might cut off the power at the governor's Granby Lakes camp, which was *his* summer White House. This didn't make any impression at all on the governor, but Richard N. Huckle found that it worked great with everybody else who used Granby Lakes Power. This was especially so after Richard N. Huckle had advanced from a lowly representative to a state Senator, at the same time becoming chairman of the Maine State Power Authority Board of Appeals and Complaints. If you had a complaint about the Granby Lakes Power Company, all you had to do was write to Richard N. Huckle at the Maine State Power Authority Board of Appeals and Complaints, and almost immediately an apology "form" letter was sent—which gave you ten days to send in your apology and your Social Security number.

CHAPTER

8

WE had become aware of the Granby Lakes Power Company seventeen days after we bought the Granby Lakes Hotel. We got an electric bill for $49.85 for seventeen days' worth of electricity used. And this was before we had the power turned on and were still back in Honansville, Connecticut, packing and getting ready for the journey to our new home in Maine.

I wrote to the Granby Lakes Power Company and suggested that we would welcome (?) electric bills from them, but only after we had used some of their electricity—or was it customary to pay in advance?

A month went by and I received no answer, but the Granby Lakes Power Company sent us another bill (or, to be more exact, two bills in one). This bill was for seventeen days and one month's use of electricity, and amounted to $88.53, and would I kindly send my check immediately.

I wrote to the Granby Lakes Power Company again. Again no reply. This nettling situation went on for two more months. By this time the bill was for $176.64 and we had yet to have the electricity turned on, or so we thought as we arrived in Granby Lakes with our kids, furniture, and animals. At last we were in our lovely hotel, which was also to be our home for the rest of our lives (my life, at least).

From the distinctly unfriendly tone of their last threat, I anticipated that the electric power would be a question of "maybe." Maybe it would be turned on and maybe it would be turned off. I flipped a switch. It was on. I thought this was sweet. They weren't monsters after all. Not until the next day anyway. But it was through the Granby Lakes Power Company that I first became acutely aware of Mr. Thomas E. Yates, the owner of the Fungo Springs Golf Course, and prince of a fellow. From the Connecticut branch of Princes of Fellows.

When Reiko and I first saw the Granby Lakes Hotel, that's all we saw. We did not notice the neighborhood, mainly because it was not in a neighborhood. It stood majestically alone high atop a small mountain with sweeping views of north, south, east, and west—with nothing blocking the lovely panorama of lakes, mountains, and thousands of square miles of pine, spruce, and birch trees. Here and there the open slopes were dotted with tiny houses attached to monstrous barns, the barns were relics of the days when the barns were stacked with tottering forty-foot-high pyramids of sweetly scented, freshly mown hay. Today they were still filled to their sway-backed ceilings not with hay but with antiques. Antiques which were shipped up daily during the tourist season from the down-country antique factories. There wasn't a barn in all of northern New England that didn't have at least eight beds that Benedict Arnold slept in. A bed that Washington had slept in would have been better, but everybody, including the unwariest of tourists, knew that Washington never got this far, while Benedict Arnold did. So the antique barn dealers, even though Benedict Arnold was not exactly an Eagle Scout in later life, felt that a ratfink general was better than no general at all, and as the historical societies put forth: "He *did* walk from Bangor to Quebec in the middle of January!" This was during the Revolutionary War, and Benedict Arnold made this famous walk from Bangor to Quebec because he wanted to surprise the British. It's just too bad that the British picked that particular time to walk from Quebec to Bangor—to surprise Benedict Arnold. The two groups passed each other on the way. They even waved as they passed.

"Who are those nuts?" both sides wondered.

But I am getting away from the theme. The theme being that we, in the excitement and thrill of the moment of arrival, had forgotten that the Fungo Springs Golf Course was directly across from our hotel. Separated only by our driveway. A glass crash and a golf ball rolling across the living room floor, followed by a large fat man, a moment later, puffing into the room, followed by a caddy, reminded us. The large fat man ignored Reiko, Bobby, Timothy, and me crouching in the corner.

"Which club do you use to get outa this living room?" he asked the caddy. The caddy suggested a seven iron, and opened the front door. It cost the large fat man three strokes, but he finally made it out of our living room and back onto the course.

"He didn't even say 'excuse me,'" Reiko said. I tried to answer her, but what I had to say was drowned in an uproar—caused by the passage of seven or eight cars of all descriptions barreling past our front door and coming to a shrieking halt in front of the Fungo Springs "pro" shop which was fifty or so yards down the road—a road that carried on after our driveway left off.

After the dust had settled in our living room and we were able to see each other again, Reiko said, "What is this—what's going on around here?"

"I think we're in the middle of a General Motors test track," Bobby said.

"Yeah," Timothy said, "—Atlas tires."

People were piling out of the cars that had just jetted by our place. "I think they're golfers," I said. "They're carrying clubs."

"Maybe they're just gonna kill snakes," Bobby suggested, bringing himself closer to the garrote.

"I'm calling that pro shop and asking them what the hell!" I said.

"Yeah?" A voice answered at the Fungo Springs Golf Course pro shop. The voice was not one of warmth or interest.

"Is this the Fungo Springs pro shop?"

"What number did you dial?" The voice had sharpened to the hard edge of insolence.

"This is Jack Douglas at the hotel. Would you kindly ask your customers to use your own driveway—and also tell them to be very careful when driving golf balls toward the hotel. We just got a golf ball in the living room."

There was a long silence after this, intermingled with the sound of chewing. Then the voice again, this time unfriendly to the point of challenge: "We got a right to use your driveway, same as you, and any golf balls in your living room gotta be returned. Any more ques-

59

tions, talk to Mr. Yates." The voice hung up. Reiko looked at me questioningly.

"Well?"

"We are living across the road from a prick," I said.

"We always do," Reiko said.

"He said they got a right to use our driveway."

"Why?" Reiko said. "They have their own driveway. Why would they want to use ours, too?"

"I'll ask Mr. Grimshaw in the morning. All it says in the deed is that Thomas E. Yates was to be allowed to pick up his golf balls on our property—it doesn't say a goddamn thing about his using our driveway for his race driver customers!" Little did I know then what we were up against, in the form of this prince of a fellow.

To this day, I have never met Thomas E. Yates, and I intend to keep it that way. It seems that he, according to Jock Lee, the owner of Granby Lakes' only saloon, is a pipe-smoking, off-the-rack Harvard male Caucasian without visible means of support except the Radcliffe girl he married. Also, according to Jock, both Thomas E. Yates and his wife have tweed blood.

On our first night in our Granby Lakes Hotel, which I wanted to rename the Honeymoon Mountain Inn because that's what it seemed like on our first idyllic evening there, we forgot all about the unpleasantness of the day as we sat out on the observation deck in the soft mountain air. From high atop our mountain we looked out over the immense expanse of Granby Lake which was shimmeringly phosphorescent with the light of an almost full moon. Reiko and I and Bobby and Timothy sat quietly, for once too entranced to argue about anything. God, I thought, what a lovely, lovely thing we have done. Moving up to this earthly paradise. This

60

heavenly haven. This radiant shore. The telephone rang.

"I'll get it," Bobby volunteered, surprisingly. Reiko and Timothy and I accepted this and just sat staring out at all this pristine beauty, trying to absorb it, to keep forever. We had almost succeeded, when Bobby announced that the Granby Lakes Power Company was on the line. How they knew we had moved in was a mystery—at that point in time.

Virgil Beam of the Granby Lakes Power Company informed me that he would be over in the morning to collect the $176.64 we owed and that, if we didn't pay, he'd be obliged to cut off our power and also sue us, and I don't know what else. This, of course, put an end to any dreamy thoughts I might have had for later on that evening.

Reiko nodded at the shack down the road. "The lights are on in the golf pro shop." I had to admit that they were. It seemed from where we sat on our deck to be very well lighted, also with spotlights on the outside of the shop.

"What the hell do they need all that light for?" I said.

"They seem to be doing something," Bobby said. "Oh, I know, they got those battery-powered golf carts."

"So what?" I said.

"That's what they're doing—they're charging the batteries in all those golf carts."

"Gee," Reiko said. "They must have at least twenty of them."

"Lot of golf carts for a crummy little course," I said, then everything became explosively clear. Why hadn't I thought about this before? Oh, wow!

"Honey, you and Bobby and Timothy watch the pro

shop—I'll be right back." I went to the little room in back of the kitchen and pulled the main electric power switch. The lights immediately doused all over the hotel. I threaded my way through a tumble of boxes, furniture, bicycles, and several pairs of tangled skis, to the observation deck. Toward the pro shop there wasn't a light to be seen.

"At last!" I said. "I'll be right back—you keep watching the pro shop."

This time I kept pulling the main electric switch off and on, off and on. I did this for a full five minutes. Then, leaving the power on, I went back to the observation deck.

"Gee," Bobby said, "there was an awful lot of yelling over at the pro shop!"

"Yeah," Reiko agreed, "and the lights kept going off and on. Gee, for a long time."

"I know," I said. "Apparently Mr. Thomas E. Yates, the owner of the Fungo Springs Golf Course, learned *something* at Harvard."

"What's that, Papa?" Bobby said.

"He learned how to tap electricity off of somebody else's meter."

Reiko laughed. "Mr. Yates wouldn't do anything like that!" But, as strange as it seems, Mr. Yates did just that. I went outside with a flashlight .and traced the illegal wire which was tapped directly into the overhead cable that fed power to the hotel. This explained those bills I had been getting from the Granby Lakes Power Company all those months. They were all metered by our meter.

I wrote to Mr. Thomas E. Yates at his Connecticut address, enclosing all the bills his pro shop had run up. In

no time at all, Mr. Thomas E. Yates indignantly returned them and informed me that in his opinion I
would not be considered an asset to the Granby Lakes
area because I apparently did not have "The Granby
Lakes Spirit," which, I thought, was about the most
unique alibi yet for not paying your bills. I wrote him a
congratulatory note, but he never answered.

CHAPTER

9

"WE gotta have a seven-hundred-and-fifty-dollar deposit from you folks," Virgil Beam of the Granby Lakes Power Company goon squad announced without any preliminaries. Virgil Beam, I guessed, had an IQ about three points lower than that of a newt defective. He had been sent over by Richard N. Huckle to extort this sum from us, in order to establish some sort of a basis for the Granby Lakes Power Company to use in assessing our ability to pay.

"A seven-hundred-and-fifty-dollar deposit?" I couldn't believe it. "When will you give it back?"

Virgil Beam pulled himself together with difficulty and said, "Oh—that depends."

"On what?"

"I dunno—they didn't tell me that part."

"Oh," I said. "And what kind of interest does the Granby Lakes Power Company pay—on my seven-hundred-and-fifty-dollars?"

Virgil Beam had to consult his little green book on this one. I got a glimpse of his little green book—the pages were blank. And so was the look on Virgil Beam's face. "What was the question?" he wanted desperately to know.

"Shit!" I said. This prompted Virgil to consult his little green book again, then he remembered. "Oh," he said, "I got here a bill for one hundred seventy-six dollars and sixty-four cents—it's for you."

"No, it isn't," I said. "It isn't for us—it's for the folks who live down the lane." Then I led him outside and gave him a little shove in the direction of the Fungo Springs pro shop, and after he was steadily on his way I went back into the living room.

Ten minutes later, Virgil Beam was back. "Mr. Yates, manager, says you don't have the Granby Lakes spirit."

"I know," I said, "I can't afford it."

Thomas E. Yates refused to pay for the power he had tapped off our line and has not paid to this day. He also informed me by letter that if I didn't stop annoying him he would not let us use our driveway. I did not, at that time, know what he meant by this. He also informed me that he would not allow us to use his well water to fill our hotel swimming pool. This was a red herring. It was Yates who was using *our* well to water his golf greens. That was something else he had learned in Cambridge—deviousness. He had various other mystical and vague threats, but I marked him as a paranoiac and I tried to ignore the ridiculous fact that our future and happiness were being threatened by a golf course.

When we bought the Granby Lakes Hotel-Motel, we reasoned—soundly enough, after we had heard all the horror stories of its tragic past—that maybe the change of name might help. Bobby wanted to call it Star Trek, Timothy was in favor of Captain Kangaroo, and Reiko wanted to call it The Teahouse of the August Moon North, which I thought might run up our printing bill when we had new brochures made. I wanted a name that was both romantic and practical and that would inspire everybody to walk out on their jobs and rush right up to Maine and spend the rest of the summer quietly luxuriating in a shade of a giant coconut palm beside our elegant free-form swimming pool, sipping an occasional sip of absinthe and 7-Up from a cool twenty-four-ounce glass—served by a nude Raquel Welch serving wench balancing a cocktail tray on her Carol Doda silicone breasts and singing "I got rhythm—who could ask for anything more?" at the same time.

All this was the impossible dream, and I knew it. There were no coconut palm trees in Maine. Absinthe was something that had been banned ever since Toulouse-Lautrec had shortened his height three feet by imbibing too much of the stuff. A twenty-four-ounce glass was not impossible to come by, but nude Raquel Welch-type serving wenches with Carol Doda breasts were as rare in Maine as coconut palms.

Any female who served drinks in the Granby Lakes area would certainly not do it in the nude—because they couldn't. They were sewn into thermal underwear on the day they were born and that was that. Their husbands and other lovers never asked questions. They assumed that every normal female had red-flannel skin with a reinforced, double-stitched copper-riveted crotch.

The more unsophisticated of the young marrieds never found out that two of the copper rivets were actually buttons—which could be unbuttoned if need be. They lived in a permanent state of tension and frustration. They knew there was something they could be doing, but thermal underwear rarely came with instructions, so they lived out their lives in quiet desperation. Two buttons away from the Big Mac of heavenly twitteration.

66

"I like Teahouse of the August Moon North!" Reiko shouted during one of our more peaceful discussions about what we were going to call our newly acquired ho-tel-motel.

I said, "Darling, just because we once appeared in a summer theater production of *Teahouse* doesn't justify its use now: besides, nobody but us and Irv Kupcinet remembers [the summer theater was in Chicago, and Irv thought we were "adequate"]—and if we call it a tea-house, people won't know we also serve booze. That's where the money is. You buy a bottle for six dollars, and you sell it for twenty-four dollars—24 drinks in every bottle. That's four hundred percent profit."

"You can get six cups of tea from every teabag, and a teabag only costs one and a half cents."

"For booze you can charge a dollar a drink. How much can you charge for a cup of tea?"

"How about fifteen cents? Six times fifteen is ninety cents—for only a cent and a half cost. That's like nine thousand percent profit—lot better than booze!"

I thought it's tough enough to reason with an American girl, and here I was trying to get through to an Oriental who by this time was American *and* Oriental. The odds were fantastic!

One month later—to the day—we settled on a name for the hotel-motel permanently. We changed it from the Granby Lakes Hotel to Honeymoon Mountain Inn, which I thought told the story pretty much. If you weren't honeymooners, maybe you'd be inspired to try to recapture that old black magic. Maybe not. But at least it was an improvement over "Granby Lakes Hotel." No-body in the village of Granby Lakes was happy about the new name. In fact, some of them became decidedly grim about the whole thing and would not acknowledge my shy smile and cheery good mornings when I went down to pick up the mail and the morning paper and a dozen doughnuts from Dolly's Doughnut Dive.

This did not bother us. Someone told us that it takes twenty-six years for the Granby Lakes people to accept you. This gave us twenty-five years and ten months to go. I felt that if I worked at it real hard, it might take only fifteen or sixteen years—and by that time most of the population of Granby Lakes would have passed to their just reward, and the younger generation would be so busy with their copper rivets, they wouldn't give a damn anyway. Besides, so far as I was concerned, there wasn't one person in the whole village who didn't accept me immediately when they saw my Bangor bankroll. (A dollar bill wrapped around a cucumber.) (Bear with me—this is a big joke in Bangor.)

The day we decided to repaint the sign, which was out on the main highway between Skowhegan and Smuggler's Notch, was a memorable one—for us. And the residents of Granby Lakes. This was the day we met Mr. Thomas E. Yates, or, I should say, one of Mr. Thomas E. Yates' representatives—by name, Oscar Moog. Mr. Moog could only be described in one way—he wasn't no Henry Kissinger.

"Hey, whaddya think you're doin'?" Mr. Moog inquired. He inquired from twenty-five feet below me on the ground and shook the frail aluminum ladder I was clinging to as I was painting out the Granby Lakes Hotel sign in preparation for its change of name and, I hoped, its image.

"Christ!" I screamed. "What the hell are *you* doing?" Mr. Moog gave the shaky ladder another rattle, which brought me down two rungs at a time. I was breathing through my mouth when I faced this ladder-shaking bastard.

"You better get this sign outa here," Mr. Moog said, jutting his receded chin—as much as it could jut—in my direction.

"What do you mean—get this sign outa here? It's my sign! I paid for it!"

"Maybe so," was the smug rejoinder, "but it's on Mr. Yates' property and he wants you to move it!"

"I'm sorry," I said, "I bought this sign and the property it's on."

"That's what you think," Mr. Moog said, whipping out a copy of our deed. "Take a look," he said, pointing to some very small print (all deeds are in very small print). "Right here—you bought a sign lot—"

"I know, I know, and this is it, right here where the sign is. Where the hell else would a sign lot be but under a sign—right?"

"Wrong." Mr. Moog was enjoying himself. "Here's the map—your sign lot is up on the corner—"

"You mean behind all those goddamn pine trees?" I managed—because the map that Mr. Moog was shoving at me might have been of the backside of the moon for all I knew. "What's the sign doing here if that's the sign lot?"

"I don't know. This sign has been here for twenty years that I know of."

"Then why do I have to move it now?"

"I don't know that either, but that's what Mr. Yates tells every new owner."

"Oh," I said, smelling the tang of a little blackmail. "If I pay off, Mr. Yates will let the sign stay here?"

"I didn't say that," Mr. Moog said.

This then was the second or third or fourth beginning of a blood feud between Mr. Thomas E. Yates and me.

"Who owns that big sign out on the highway?" Reiko asked Egil Grimshaw, in his office on Main Street. We ran to Egil Grimshaw now with every problem, big or small, because he was never ruffled or distraught by anything (that happened to *us*).

"My dear," Egil said, at his silkiest best, "you do. It's your sign—it advertises your hotel. How could there be any question as to whom the sign belongs?"

"I'm glad to hear that," I said.

"Of course," Egil Grimshaw said, "that sign has advertised the Granby Lakes Hotel for thirty years."

"But," Reiko said, "we wanted to change the sign—paint a different name on it. Can we do that?"

"Of course, my dear," Egil said, thumbing his baby-blue suspenders, "paint anything you want on it. I repeat, it's your sign."

"But," I said, "Mr. Yates claims it's on his property."

"It is," Egil Grimshaw said, "it is."

There was a long period of silence after this. Neither Reiko nor I knew what to say. Egil Grimshaw knew what to say, but he didn't say it. Then, after what seemed like a week and a half, I said, "Well, there's no problem then, is there?"

"Of course not," Egil said. "Just move the sign up the road five or six hundred feet—onto *your* sign lot. How could there be any trouble?"

CHAPTER

10

IT took the contractor, who was highly recommended by Egil Grimshaw, almost two weeks to move our sign to our sign lot. The sign—which did not look massive when viewed from the road, driving by— weighed almost five thousand pounds (not counting the footings of poured concrete that had to be broken away, piece by piece, before the steel legs holding the sign could be uprooted).

The contractor, whom Grimshaw had highly recommended, seemed to be in an eternal stupor. The simplest questions were never answered, and we didn't dare ask the more complex questions, like "When the hell are you gonna finish this job, Mr. Fronton?"

We complained to Egil Grimshaw. "Don't worry about old Fronton," Egil said. "He's slow, but by God he's sure."

"About what?" I wanted to know.

"Huh?" Egil said.

"I said—Old Fronton is sure about what?"

"Oh, about what he's doing—very reasonable, too."

Old Fronton's idea of "very reasonable" changed the whole ratio of our nest egg. When we'd paid Old Fronton's fee for moving the sign, we had more nest than egg. The fee we had agreed on turned out to be only the beginning. We hadn't been told about the little extras: like dynamiting holes for the new sign site; the hiring of a derrick with a six-man crew to hoist the sign (one man worked the derrick—the other five prayed that the cable wouldn't snap). The cable snapped and all six of them said, "Well, I'll be goddamned!" The Pope, the Archbishop of Canterbury, and the late Lester Maddox couldn't have prayed as a trio enough to keep that ancient cable from snapping.

The cable snapped fifteen times before they got the sign moved, and I thought it was a miracle that none of the workmen had been hurt by the viciously lashing steel rope. The men were intact at the end of the job, but, on the final hoist, the cable snapped for the last time. The workmen were still unscathed, but the derrick was sliced in half. It looked like a commercial for Zeibart rust-proofing as narrated by Rod Serling.

After our sign had been repainted from "Granby Lakes Hotel" to "Honeymoon Mountain Inn," we sat back and waited for the flow of eager customers. The flow turned out to be not a trickle. Not nobody. Except Mr. DeVoe. Mr. DeVoe had the unpleasant habit of Lavoris breath and early rising, and at seven A.M. one rosy morning thumped on our front door with his book of rules. Mr. DeVoe turned out to be the health inspector for the district. It was his duty to see that hotels and motels and filling station washrooms were kept relatively neat and tidy and Lysolized. When I opened the door, still in part of my pajamas, with my hair and brains very much tousled, Mr. DeVoe's first words were, "I'm here to check your water." My first impulse was to piss all over him and say, "There it is—check it." I didn't, but I had the feeling that someday I would. I invited him in and asked him if he'd like a cup of coffee. He said he'd have to check my water first. Again I wanted to do what I had wanted to do.

Mr. DeVoe marched into the kitchen and proceeded to turn on his professionalism by testing a nice clean glass of artesian well water with various strange-looking vials of colored liquids. Finally, after much humming and "aha's," he said, "Bad news."

"Bad news? What kind of bad news?"

"You got a lot of hydrogen and oxygen in your water."

"Oh," I said, relieved, "isn't that—the idea?"

"What do you mean?" Mr. DeVoe was suddenly on the defensive.

"I mean," I said, loftily, "that water is composed of two parts of hydrogen and one part of oxygen."

"That may be, Mr. Douglas"—Mr. DeVoe was even more belligerent than formerly—"but you got the wrong proportions."

My gorge was rising fast. "We've been drinking that water for the past six months!"

"Might just as well be drinking whale piss!" Mr. DeVoe yelled back.

"What does whale piss consist of?" I wanted to know. "What's the formula?"

"Cesium, lutetium, lactatorum, arsenite, halogen, and thorium," Mr. DeVoe said, smiling like a Cheshire cheese.

The son of a bitch, I thought. He either knows or else he knows that I haven't the slightest knowledge of this type of seagoing urination and just threw a lot of chemical-sounding names at me hoping I'd buy it. I bought it. I had no choice.

"What can I do about our water?" I said, knowing what the answer was going to be.

"Nothing," he said, "nothing. If you want potable water—water you can serve to your customers—when you hopefully ha!ha!—have some, you will have to drill a new well, and maybe, just *maybe,* of course, you may get good water."

I knew as long as we insisted on hanging onto our dubiously good investment, we would never get water that would pass any test that Mr. DeVoe's magic chemical set would let get by. So far as he and Granby Lakes were concerned, we had had it—in the water department.

We had neither the money nor the intention of drilling a new well, and sensing this, Mr. DeVoe said, "If you serve—even so much as one glass of this filthy stuff— we'll have to fine you a thousand dollars or one year in jail or both."

"That bad, huh?"

"Yeah, and them county jails ain't no picnic grounds."

I couldn't resist. "What do they do in them no-picnic-grounds jails—make them New Hampshire 'Live Free or Die' license plates?"

"Wait and see," Mr. DeVoe said, jamming his chemical bottles and vials and syringes into his doctor bag. Without another word, he slammed the door after him.

Again we rushed to Egil Grimshaw's side to seek his excellent advice and warm consolation. What the hell could we do about this implacable health inspector? We couldn't afford a new well.

"How do you know you can't afford a new well?" Egil asked. "The cost may be a lot less than you envision."

"Jesus H. Christ!" I said. "No matter what the cost— we just can't cut it!"

74

"Well," Egil said, without much hope, and rubbing his baby-blue suspenders until they purred, "you can't expect people to drink water that isn't potable."

"What's 'potable'?" Reiko wanted to know.

"I just happen to know a well driller that's free at the moment. You're really in luck," Egil said. "And you can't have people going around saying that you are serving poisoned water!"

"Who's saying that?"

"Well, almost everybody."

I started to yell again, "*Everybody!* We haven't seen a soul since we opened!"

"Well," Egil Grimshaw counseled, "I'd get ahold of Old Fronton right now while he isn't busy—I'd get that well going as soon as possible."

This first was only one of quite a few visits we had from Mr. DeVoe; it seems that he was also the county fire inspector. And we didn't come out too well in that either. Although the house had been used as a hotel for fifty or sixty or whatever number of years, it had never passed the fire inspection. Because it was made of wood.

"Did you ever see that hotel they have in Poland Spring, Maine?" I asked, referring, of course, to the Poland Spring Hotel, which was older than ours and made of wood and had been used as a hotel for longer than ours. To this day it has not burned down, and it passes the fire inspection every year.

"That's different," Mr. DeVoe said.

"Why? Why is the Poland Spring Hotel any different than ours—it's about twenty times bigger—maybe more—"

"*Thirty* times bigger—and it's made of wood."

"Then what the hell is the difference?" I said, not too sweetly, I hoped.

"The Poland Spring Hotel is owned by a local boy."

"Sol Feldman is the owner of the Poland Spring Hotel, and happens to be a friend of mine—*he's* a local boy?"

"An *honorary* local boy."

"Oh," I said, "you can make adjustments in your social system to meet any requirement—right?"

"You're getting the picture, huh?" Mr. DeVoe said, his eyes merrily twinkling—like a jolly cobra, toying with an unmanly mongoose.

"You mean—because this hotel is made out of wood—we are going to fail your fire inspection test?"

"Don't be silly—you just have to make a few minor changes." Then Mr. DeVoe started to give me the list of the few minor changes. A new sprinkler system, steel double doors on all the rooms, a fire warning signal, and a direct line to the firehouse. (This was pretty funny because the firehouse had burned down eight years before—with the hand-pumper in it—and it had never been replaced.) To continue with the list of what we were to have to pass the fire inspection would take three more chapters and cost us more money than World War II (one of our cheaper wars).

I told Mr. DeVoe that we would see what we could do, and he threatened us again with the thousand-dollar fine, the year in jail, or both—and left, again, slamming the door.

One month later on a zero-cold November day, when he didn't hear the sound of hammering coming from

The Honeymoon Mountain Inn, he showed up again, as the county liquor inspector. Needless to say, our liquor did not pass inspection. When I asked him why, he said, "The alcoholic content of your vodka is too high—it's one hundred proof."

Reiko, who had been acting as bartender, agreed that it was one hundred proof. "That's the way it comes—from the liquor store."

"Where did you buy this stuff," Mr. DeVoe said suspiciously, "out of state? Liquor is much cheaper out of state, and higher proof."

"We know that," I said.

"Oh, then you admit it?"

"Mr. DeVoe," I said, "you are beginning to bug me. We bought that bottle of one-hundred-proof vodka at the state liquor store in *this* state. I have the receipt right here—" I showed him the blue sheet, which is the sheet the Maine state liquor-license holder gets when he buys his liquor at the Maine State Bureau of Alcoholic Beverages liquor store.

"I'll be goddamned!" he said.

"You will by me," I said, "if you don't get off our backs."

Mr. DeVoe took this in stride. "This bottle here," he said, "has been watered."

"That's *water,*" I said, and it was. Bobby and Timothy had been playing bartender and customer all afternoon with a Scotch bottle filled with water. They'd been taking turns portraying a Granby Lakes drunk.

"That does it!" Mr. DeVoe said, licking his overdeveloped chops. "We gotcha! Serving this polluted water you were warned against serving! One thousand dollars fine or one year in jail—or both—now *what* will it *be?*"

Well, it was neither—on his way back to report us, Mr. DeVoe rode his snowmobile over a weak place in the ice in the very middle of Granby Lake, and just like *that* the county needed a new water, fire, and liquor inspector.

CHAPTER

11

WITH the sudden demise of Mr. DeVoe—the liquor, fire, and water inspector—we knew we'd be safe only momentarily. Our state, we were becoming more aware, was not in short supply of incompetent martinet bureaucrats.

"Let's forget Mr. DeVoe," Reiko suggested, "and get on with fixing this place up."

I really couldn't forget Mr. DeVoe because he and his Skidoo were still at the bottom of the lake, and I had made plans to salvage his Skidoo. No one had plans to salvage Mr. DeVoe.

There was so much that needed doing, which, of course, we hadn't noticed when we bought our hotel. We were blinded by the magnificent view and deafened by the continual stream of wild praise and promises pouring forth from the mouths of Miss Hinkley and Egil Grimshaw. Praise about what we were getting and promises of vast riches and unimaginable rewards to come through our ownership of our very own Honeymoon Mountain Inn.

"I think the first thing to do would be to paint the place," Reiko said.

"You think it needs paint? I love those gray-weathered old shingles."

"Those gray-weathered old shingles are not gray-weathered at all. They've been painted gray with some very cheap paint." This came as a shock. I thought they were cedar and had weathered to a lovely shade of gray as cedar shingles do, but, upon close examination, Reiko was right. They weren't cedar. I couldn't tell what kind of wood they were. I wasn't even sure they were wood. They looked like some sort of cardboard that had been soaked in the curative waters of Lake Erie and had died along with it.

Reiko and I were not yet aware that the forces of evil were working against us and the Honeymoon Mountain Inn—and its chances of anything approaching success —so we asked Egil Grimshaw to put us in touch with a good painter and also someone who could lay carpet. As usual, Egil Grimshaw dropped whatever charitable project he was working on at the time (organizing an Easter sunrise crap game for the Granby Lakes VFW, he told us) and scurried around and came up with one Corky Mulligan of Mulligan Interiors, "who's the best carpet layer in Maine," and one Ferd Macoomb, "who's the best house painter in all of New England."

We had no way of checking the credentials of either of these two worthies, so we hired them, and I think anyone reading this knows *what* is coming. And you're right.

We had bought carpet at some twenty dollars per yard, which we wanted laid wall to wall in our huge living room. The carpet was beige and it was beautiful.

After instructing Corky Mulligan of Mulligan Interiors exactly how we wanted this wall-to-wall carpet to look, Reiko and I and the kids took off for Bangor to see if we could find a gallon of real Maine maple syrup before it became extinct. Also we wanted to be out of Corky Mulligan's way while he worked.

The six-hour trip (there and back) to Bangor proved to be a failure. No one in Bangor had ever heard of maple syrup.

"What's it made of?" one colorful Maine character wanted to know.

"It's from a tree," Bobby volunteered, which I knew would terminate any understanding we might have built up with this colorful Maine character.

"No, no, sonny." The colorful Maine character spoke right up. "You got it wrong—pulp is made from a tree, and International Paper's got the whole thing sewed up."

The trip back to Granby Lakes was uneventful except for the usual back-seat riots between Bobby and Timothy punctuated by my Three-Stooges-type backhand slaps across their chocolate-smeared mouths, and insulting admonitions from Reiko about my driving ability.

As we pulled up in front of the Honeymoon Mountain Inn, we all quieted down in anticipation of the joy of seeing our lovely living room carpeted wall to wall in the soft pure wool of our twenty-dollar-per-yard carpeting.

We threw open the front door and there it was—our three hundred square yards of priceless (almost) wall-to-wall carpeting! Christ! We couldn't believe it! Each precious piece of carpet had been overlapped and nailed down onto the next precious section. The effect was of a beige Japanese farm, terraced for rice planting.

"What the hell is this?!" I said to the smiling proprie-

81

tor of Mulligan Interiors, who was lolling in one of our Eames chairs drinking a large slug of Chivas Regal from our bar.

"Like it?" Mulligan said. "Wall to wall, like you said."

"Wall to wall my ass!" I screamed.

"If you say so," Mulligan made as if to get up. "Plenty of carpet left over."

"Sit down, folks," Egil Grimshaw invited us kindly. Egil was on the phone. "Yeah, that sounds good, Elmer. If he don't pay up, put a lien on his whole cemetery. Yeah, see you at vespers." Egil hung up, "Just getting our March of Nickels campaign under way," he explained.

"March of nickels?"

"Yeah, that's the best we can do here in Maine —raised seventy-six dollars and thirty-five cents last year—bought cranberry sauce for the poor at Thanksgiving. They had to provide their own turkeys. Now what can I do for you folks? Carpet man work out okay, like I said he would? Good man, Mulligan. Now what can I do for you folks—before I go to choir practice?"

"Mulligan is an incompetent no-good bastard!" I said.

"True enough," Egil agreed, "but you can't beat him when it comes to laying carpets."

The house painter whom Egil Grimshaw recommended had skin so transparent you could almost see his brain not working, but Egil said that Ferd Macoomb was the best. So.

"Mr. Macoomb," Reiko said, "what color do you think we ought to paint the place?"

"Well," Mr. Macoomb said, shit-kicking imaginary shit on our living-room floor, "depends on what they got on sale down to The Farmers Co-op—down to Green's Corners."

"I don't quite understand," I said, although I understood perfectly. Have you ever wondered why—driving through the New England countryside—you see so many weirdly colored houses? Houses painted green in front, yellow and blue on the sides, with red, white, and pink shutters? They were having a sale down to Green's Corners. That's why.

"Paint's much cheaper when it's on sale," Mr. Macoomb said, reasonably.

"But," Reiko said, "supposing they don't have the color you want—on sale. What then?"

"Well"—Mr. Macoomb snorted at this weird reasoning—"if you're *fussy!*"

I jumped in quickly. "It's not that, Mr. Macoomb," I said. "It's just that we want to paint the Honeymoon Mountain Inn a color that will please the people around here—after all, we're strangers and—"

"Oh." Mr. Macoomb laughed. "You won't be strangers long—twenty-five, thirty years, you'll be just like—acquaintances." I looked to see if he was pulling our legs in a sly down-east fashion, but he wasn't. He meant just what he said, and I knew it would take at least that long before the natives of Granby Lakes would accept us. Not that they had ever accepted anyone who had owned the old Granby Lakes Hotel, so the whole thing was academic or moot or both.

"Well," Reiko said, "I think we should paint the place gray with red window trim."

"Gray—with red window trim." Mr. Macoomb committed this to memory, then: "What kinda paint were you figuring on?"

"Well," I sort of chuckled-sniggered, "we thought we'd leave that up to you."

"Oh?" Mr. Macoomb was quite pleased at this, although we didn't know why at the time.

"Okay if I start this here coming Monday?" he said.

"Fine," Reiko and I both said. This was a lot sooner than we thought. "Will you have time to get the paint and everything you need by then?"

"Oh, don't worry about that," Mr. Macoomb said. "I'm goin' fishing down near Green's Corners this Saturday, and I can pick the paint up then. Fishing's pretty good on the Avery Creek—runs right through Green's Corners—"

"Good, good—don't forget the paint," I said, feeling that as usual around this part of the country, everything gets sidetracked or forgotten if the fish are biting.

"Don't you worry about that," Mr. Macoomb said. "White—with blue window trim. Couldn't forget that."

After we got Mr. Macoomb straightened out on the colors—with the aid of a couple more Chivas Regals—he climbed into his pickup truck and careened down the hill—I hoped in the direction of his home—or Green's Corners.

Mr. Macoomb proved to be the fastest house painter alive, although I felt that he should have cleaned off a lot more of the ages of accumulated grime that covered the shingles and the window trim first.

"Don't worry about it, Mr. D. This paint will cover

anything!" And I'll have to admit—it did. We also had the blessing of clear sunny days all the time Mr. Macoomb was whizzing through his task.

We were very pleased with the results of Mr. Macoomb's efforts. The Honeymoon Mountain Inn looked brand-new. We fell in love with it all over again. After we paid Mr. Macoomb what seemed to be a fair sum, not a bargain by any means, but fair for the good job he had done, we gave him a whole bottle of Chivas to take home with him (we felt that was better than having him drink it on the premises—which he would have done with the slightest urging).

"Finally," Reiko said, "we got a good job done by somebody in Granby Lakes. I never thought it would happen."

"Neither did I. I still can't believe it."

That night it rained. The next morning The Honeymoon Mountain Inn was sitting in the center of five acres of gray grass—with a border of red trim. Mr. Macoomb had used water paint. Eight hundred dollars' worth.

CHAPTER

12

"WELL, I've got it all figured out," Thunker Shill, the insurance man, said (Thunker was his nickname), "and very reasonable, too. I cut down wherever I could." This was good news because we were cutting down wherever we could, too. We had cut out steak entirely, and gasoline I mixed: two parts regular and one part vermouth. This was a lot cheaper than Premium.

"How much will the insurance cost us?" Reiko asked, as usual getting right to the point.

"Only twenty-seven hundred thirteen dollars and forty-two cents." Thunker Shill beamed. I thought he was going to get up and take a bow, he was so pleased with himself.

"So what does that amount to—per year?" I asked.

"Only twenty-seven hundred thirteen dollars and forty-two cents."

Reiko and I just looked at each other. What we had here was a madman—selling insurance. Or maybe, more accurately, a slicker—a con man—a crafty cat. Thunker Shill sensed he had gone a bit too far.

"I tried to give you what you asked me for," he said, removing a colored handkerchief from his breast pocket and starting to twist it nervously. "I gave you one hundred and ten thousand dollars on the main house and—"

"One hundred and ten thousand dollars on the main house! Jesus! It's only worth forty or forty-five at the most! I told you that right from the beginning—six or eight months ago when you first came here!"

This was the start of something big, to quote Steve Allen. After we had barred this opportunist from Camelot forever, he threatened us with a lawsuit. The reason— he had (according to him) already insured the hotel for this horrendous amount, and he expected us to pay the premium unprotestingly, like two innocent and trusting sheep being led through Swift & Company's little green door.

I complained to the Maine State Insurance Bureau about this bald attempt to mulct us out of more than a thousand dollars of insurance premium for insurance we had not asked for and did not want.

The Maine State Insurance Bureau answered by return mail. They were very concerned, but not about us. They were shocked that we were attempting to cheat this poor Maine insurance broker out of his rightfully earned fee. A complaint (or even a query) from an out-of-stater was treated by the Maine State Insurance Bureau as both a challenge and an insult.

Our new insurance broker, Milton Strunk, was just as much a slicker as our former insurance broker, but he was so smooth we didn't realize it. He gave us a list of incidents and accidents which have happened in some resort hotels, with the intention, of course, of making us buy more insurance.

The list was horrendous:

87

At a resort hotel in Old Orchard Beach, a guest choked to death on his kazoo while playing, "Roll out the barrel and we'll have a barrel of fun."

At a resort in Skowhegan, Richard Burton fell downstairs in a one-story hotel.

At a resort hotel at Moosehead Lake, a careless whistling swan flew through an open window and right into a fat lady who was bending over the bathtub. The poor swan stopped whistling almost immediately. The fat lady sang three choruses of "I could have danced all night" before she called the management to report a strange bird.

At a resort hotel at Ogunquit, a little Frenchman and his wife and his mistress spent the whole month of July trapped in a wall bed.

"That's ridiculous," Reiko said, "they'd starve to death!"

"Oh, they did," Milton Strunk said, "but they were having so much fun they didn't notice it."

"At a resort hotel in Bar Harbor, some guy found his wife in bed with another man, so he shot the bellboy."

"I don't understand that at all," I said, "why would he shoot the bellboy?"

"Because he was in bed with his wife and the other guy."

"Up in Millinocket," Milton Strunk continued, "a very meticulous guest of this very fancy hotel found a mouse in his fried rice."

"Did he sue the hotel?" I asked like a dolt.

"He certainly did," Milton Strunk said, "and so did the mouse."

"Oh, come on now," Reiko said, not really knowing

whether Milton Strunk was kidding or not, "how could a mouse sue a hotel?"

"Easy," Milton Strunk said, "William Kunstler took the case."

"Look," I said, "let's stop having fun—if that's what we're doing—"

"Okay," Milton Strunk said, "you've got about eighty thousand dollars' worth of fire insurance, plus the one-million-dollar personal catastrophe policy, which costs a little extra."

"How much extra?" Reiko wanted to know.

"Three dollars."

"That's all?"

"Yes, and for another fifty cents—more or less—you can have the special 'Buffalo Stampede' clause. For husbands only."

"Oh, we're back to having fun, eh?" I said.

"Not at all," Milton said. "It's right here in the Great North American Casualty and Catastrophe policy. Paragraph eighty-six, Clause twelve." I read Clause twelve of Paragraph eighty-six. It read: "The widow of resort hotel guest (male) who is accidentally and irrefutably trampled to death by a buffalo stampede on July 17, 1983, will not only receive ten thousand ($10,000) in cash, but also she will have a choice of an 8-x-10 Polaroid photo (in color) snapped by Sir Laurence Olivier right after his being trampled by the herd of buffalo, *or* the Company will send him home (vulcanized and gift-wrapped) so the widow may use him as an extra bathmat."

I didn't say a word after I read this, but I thought, *we've got another madman on our hands.* Suddenly Milton Strunk shrieked with hysterical laughter. His face

89

turned red and he started pounding the coffee table with his fist.

"Gotcha again, didn't I?!" he whooped.

"Look," I said, grabbing him by his seven-inch lapels, "you're lots of fun, but settle down for Chrissakes! We've wasted enough time on this goddamn insurance. We've got other things to do!"

"So have I," Milton admitted, "but you don't know how dull it is selling this stuff—I use that phony buffalo stampede policy to relax people and to keep from going nuts myself. This is really just a sideline anyway. My real job is—I'm the owner of the Milton Strunk Paper Company—we're fighting it out with the International Paper Company and the Brown Paper Company."

"Gee," Bobby said, from nowhere, "those are pretty big outfits—that's what they teach us in the sixth grade anyway." (They teach kids this in every sixth grade in northern New England.)

I found later that Milton Strunk was indeed the owner of the Milton Strunk Paper Company, and it was very specialized, according to an item in the entertainment section of a Portland newspaper. One of the "things to do" while in Maine was visit the Milton Strunk Paper Company in Livermore Falls and watch them take three eight-foot logs and make them into one day's supply of toilet paper for every man, woman, and child in the states of Georgia, Alabama, and Tennessee, which, as some cynic pointed out, doesn't mean much because a helluva lot of people in Georgia, Alabama, and Tennessee don't know what toilet paper is. They think it's just family-size albino party streamers in an unhandy roll for throwing on New Year's Eve.

Finally, after a few more days and nights of discussion, we got what we thought was pretty good insurance coverage on the Honeymoon Mountain Inn. Also, although we didn't know it at the time, we were the first owners to ever have any insurance on the place. The former owners had "binders," and if you don't know what a "binder" is, you are part of a vast majority. Even the experts don't know. Or they won't tell you. I asked Ed Reimers of Allstate what a binder was, and he said cheese or the drinking water in Toledo.

CHAPTER

13

THE knocking on our front door had been going on for some time I thought. I was sleeping on the floor in front of the fireplace. The knocking became louder and continuous. I began to wonder why someone didn't open the door. After a while I began to think about me. Why didn't I open the door? It seemed like a lousy idea, but I got up and did it.

"Hey, you wanna buy some Girl Scout cookies?" It was little Betsy Couzy, the green-eyed pixie informer.

"How old are they?" I asked her.

"Old enough not to eat," Betsy said. "And my father says you're still a dum-dum!"

"Your father's getting more right all the time," I said. "Every day and every way—"

"You had Mulligan and Ferd Macoomb workin' for you, didn't you? And you bought some insurance from Milton Strunk?"

"You don't miss much, do you?"

"Nope—they all kickback to Grimshaw."

"What?"

"Everybody who works for you or sells you anything all kickback money to Egil Grimshaw—you didn't know, huh? Oh, hello, Mrs. Douglas—you look beautiful today." Reiko ignored this.

"What's a kickback?"

92

"It's nothing," I said, trying to spare Reiko the crass side of commercial life.

"Every time Mr. Grimshaw recommends somebody to work for you—they have to give him money," Betsy Couzy explained helpfully, like the good little Girl Scout she wasn't. Reiko swore a Japanese oath which didn't sound like an oath at all—it was cooed like the sound of a mourning dove, but it translated into "the dirty son of a bitch!" This was one of the few Japanese words I knew and I agreed.

"There's only one thing to do, I guess," I said, "and that's to have no more traffic with Egil Grimshaw—"

"I like Mr. Grimshaw," Timothy said in his five-year-old voice. "He gives me lollipops."

"Yeah," Betsy Couzy said, "he gets 'em free from Elsie's Candy Store—he's got her mortgage. And he pinches her ass all the time—it's quite a large mortgage."

After Betsy Couzy left and we were throwing two dozen Girl Scout cookies into the garbage pail before they contaminated our can of Lysol, the telephone rang. It was Egil Grimshaw and he had good news. News that blocked out any reservations we might have had about him and his far-reaching cupidity.

Egil Grimshaw had some guests who were just dying to stay at the Honeymoon Mountain Inn! I felt like giving him a twenty-one-gun salute. He suggested the best way to make money with our newly acquired hotel was to invite or encourage conventions of various ilk and inclination to "take advantage"—a phrase I'm not sure I liked—of our superb location "high in the Andes of Maine" and of the splendiferous nature of our accommodations. (We had lovely paper bathmats—with a picture of a moose being shot at three paces by a fearless hunter. This was meant to give the place a Maine flavor—like L. L. Bean and balsam-scented Preparation H.)

I should have been wary of any suggestion that Egil Grimshaw authored—because, from what little Betsy Couzy hinted, Egil Grimshaw had none of the attributes of a Grey Lady, but I let him arrange to have a group of fifty psychologists conduct a week-long "seminar" at our Honeymoon Mountain Inn. I looked up the meaning of "seminar," but it didn't help. It means a group getting together to study something, which sounded all right until they arrived. After they arrived and *I* had studied *them,* I couldn't imagine what they were here to study. Half of them were young, with children, wives, and girlfriends. They were quiet and serious and dressed conservatively. The other half was middle-aged and boisterous; they were dressed for a Truman Capote April in Paris Ball. They also had wives and girlfriends, but no children. The wives and girlfriends, it seemed, were interchangeable.

The psychologists were delightful if this is what you want out of life. I decided right then and there that week that I am not a born innkeeper—I am a born ax murderer.

Our guests were more like ants than people. There was no avoiding them—although we had our own separate, private living quarters—we thought. They were not separate and private, long. They invaded us like huns or maybe I should say like ants who had studied hunnery. We looked up one morning from our cozy little bed—Reiko, Bobby, Timothy, and me—and there they were—in our bedroom. To give them some benefit of doubt, our bedroom *had* been the hotel dining room before we had the audacity to transform it into one of the most sensational bedrooms ever. It was thirty by for-

94

ty feet, with floor to ceiling windows and a view over-looking all of Maine, which is what I wish we had done before we rashly decided to go into the hotel business. For fun. Going into the hotel business for fun is like slicing salami with a guillotine. Sooner or later you're going to miss the salami.

Our bedroom was invaded again on Saturday morning. At six A.M.—psychologists get up early or stay up all night—I never knew. Everyone was very apologetic, including me because I was naked except for my wristwatch and my West Point ring and I was kneeling on the floor facing Mecca, praying *for* the septic tank and the water pipes and *against* the mortgage interest rates.

Some of them stripped immediately and started praying with me. Others just asked what time did the bar open and left.

This was only the beginning. I had made arrangements by letter and telephone as to what areas they could use for their seminars. I gave them almost complete run of the entire place, including two guest houses, a room off the bar, and a large open basement, plus twenty acres of outdoor playground, but apparently all this unforbidden territory had no charm for them. Or maybe it was the lack of challenge. The forbidden fruit syndrome. Whatever it was, it was goddamn annoying. One gloomy August day was the day of climax. The children and I were sitting in our living room, which was also enormous with twenty-four-foot ceilings and a large fireplace at each end of the room. Each fireplace capable of burning eighty dollars' worth of firewood in an evening. Timothy was lying on the floor, looking at the split beavers in *Playboy, Oui, Penthouse, Genesis,* and *Screw,* trying to figure out what they were. Bobby was lying on the floor, looking over Timothy's shoulder, fascinated, and I was in my easy chair, staring into the darkened fireplace, wondering why they insisted on having sex education courses in school.

"What are you doing, Bobby?" I asked.

"My homework," he said.

Suddenly the room was full of weirdos. Our guests.

"May I help you," I said in a voice tonalized to mean that *help* was the very last thing they would ever get from me. This stopped them not. They all sat down in front of the fireplace and the television set which was playing full blast as an old Jimmy Cagney or Bogart gangster movie filled the room with strange and wonderful nostalgic sounds of the days that never were.

I may not have resented this intrusion too much until someone, Dr. Fink I think his name was—I *know* it was Dr. Fink (and he was aptly named if I may say so in passing)—turned off the Bogart movie and switched to an ever-popular soap opera (where everyone in it had some terminal affliction).

"Dr. Fink," I said, trying to sound like George Sanders at his snottiest, but only managing to sound like Ernest Borgnine at his suavest, "Dr. Fink, how would you like to have a sex change right here in my living room?"

This quieted things down in an instant.

"I don't think," Dr. Fink said, "I don't think I quite understand."

"Let me put it this way, Dr. Fink," I said. "This is our home and this is our living room. This is the only room in the whole hotel-motel complex where we can get away from you and your group, and if you, as leader of your group, don't lead them out of here by the time I count three, I am going to cut your cock off, have it bronzed, and shove it up your nose."

"Oh," Dr. Fink said, "what a marvelous idea for 'Let's

96

Make a Deal.' I'll pretend I'm a unicorn! Maybe I'll win a free trip to Hawaii!"

I gave up.

On the surface, this large group of well-paying guests seemed like a windfall, even after I had learned that each guest had paid Egil Grimshaw, the travel agent, and convention counselor, fifty dollars apiece for allowing them to spend a week at the Honeymoon Mountain Inn. This fifty-dollar fee, we didn't learn of until the end of their stay, at bill-paying time. They each presented a small card entitling them to a fifty-dollar reduction on their week's sojourn. The little slip of paper they presented to me with too much alacrity looked like the coupon you get in a pound of coffee or five pounds of Burgerbits, which is worth fifteen cents if you ever purchase coffee or Burgerbits again.

I called Egil Grimshaw. "What the hell is this fifty-dollar reduction bit?"

"Oh, hello there, Jack. How're things up on the hill?" Egil Grimshaw said, making "up on the hill" sound like a mental institution, which was a prelude of things to come.

"How *could* things be up here on the hill with fifty psychologists on the loose?" I said.

"Well, glad to hear business is good," Egil Grimshaw said, as a method of ringing off.

"Wait a minute," I said. "What is this fifty-dollar reduction in everyone's bill?"

"Oh," he said, "that's the usual."

"The usual what?"

"How do you think a travel agency runs, Jack—on love?"

"You get fifty dollars per person—as a fee for one

97 .

lousy week's stay at a hotel?" I said. "I could do better with the Mafia."

"That could be," he agreed. "They're much better organized, so they can cut a little here and there. Besides, Jack, you must remember, I don't get that full fifty dollars—the travel agency gets it."

"Wait a minute," I said, "you *are* the travel agency!"

"You forget Poseidon," he said.

"I never *saw* Poseidon," I said.

"Well," Egil Grimshaw said, "Poseidon is very shy, spends most of his time taking a Dale Carnegie course, wants to be able to face people." I could just picture Egil Grimshaw leaning back in his king-sized executive chair, snapping his baby-blue galluses, smiling like a fat cat full of gullible canaries, and cultivating his Maine accent—leaving the *r*'s off everything and broadening his *a* so that "barn" came out "ban" and "car" metamorphosed into "kaa." Early in the game, he had found this impressed the down-country people into believing that he was a real hick, ready to be taken by any slicker that walked into his office.

"Christ, Egil!" I said. "Fifty bucks apiece—that's twenty-five hundred dollars."

"Twenty-seven fifty," he said.

"What!"

"Ten percent tax."

"It's five percent in this state!" I screamed.

"Yeah," he agreed, "but in Granby Lakes, it's ten. It's all here in our tax brochure."

"I never saw any brochure about taxes," I said.

"I know," he said, "we keep it in the safe. No use wrecking the economy of Granby Lakes just because a few facts are not common knowledge."

98

CHAPTER

14

"I wonder what Buddha has in store for us today," Bobby, our oldest, said, during a short pause between his eighth and ninth piece of toast and jam, while he surreptitiously aimed the kick-of-death under the table at his little brother, Timothy. This set things in motion. Reiko slowed Bobby down somewhat with a motherly karate chop to the back of his neck. Timothy aimed a practice kick-of-death under the table at Bobby's crotch. Bobby screamed, although he hadn't been touched. I screamed because Timothy miscalculated and Reiko gave me a wifely karate chop and suggested I stop yelling at the breakfast table. Bobby laughed, started in on his tenth toast and jam, and aimed another kick at Timothy, and we went through the whole early morning ceremony again.

Breakfast in the lovely sunlit dining room of the Honeymoon Mountain Inn was something like the Last Supper and a Hollywood pot party, as produced, written, and directed by Mel Brooks.

I didn't know what Buddha had in store for me, but I knew it wouldn't be anything pleasant. The campaign of the village of Granby Lakes against the new owners of the Honeymoon Mountain Inn was in full swing. Reiko confirmed this with her next announcement: "Mrs. Gumpers is coming today."

"Who the hell is Mrs. Gumpers?" I said, and not just to irritate Reiko, as I sometimes do when things get dull and quiet and there's nothing on the telly but reruns of *Victory at Sea*, which has nice music, but not enough violence (compared to *Kojak*).

"Mrs. Gumpers, the maid," Timothy said, trying to eat raisin bran with one chopstick.

"Is she the maid who always turns all the lights on and not off—plus leaving the water run in the bathrooms—and who never remembers to put a fresh roll of paper on the holder?"

"That's the one," Reiko said, "and she always forgets the Kleenex and the little bars of soap and the bath towels and the face towels and the washcloths and that little strip of paper across the middle of the toilet seat."

"You know," Bobby said, turning his head carefully so as not to lose its alignment with his neck (after Reiko's vertebrae-scrambling karate chop), "nobody ever told me what's with hotels and motels—I mean, what's that little strip of paper stretched across the toilet seat supposed to do?"

"Yeah," Timothy said, "what's it supposed to do?"

"Ask your father," Reiko said, suddenly remembering that she was Japanese and not used to the ways of the West.

"I don't know what it's for," I had to confess. "All I know is it makes it damned inconvenient, if you're in a hurry. But it does give the guest a feeling of honor and immortality."

"What the hell does that mean?" Reiko said, forgetting she was a Japanese wife, all feminine and soft-talking and trying to please.

100

"To break that little strip of paper across the top of the toilet seat is like cutting a ribbon to open a new Golden Gate bridge."

"Papa's a romanticist," Bobby said.

"You bet your ass I am," I said, destroying my momentary Robert Browning image.

"I thought we couldn't say 'ass' inside the house," Timothy said. "Isn't that right, Mommie?"

Before Mommie could reply, I said, "Will you please ask Mrs. Gumpers, when and if she shows up today, not to flush the Tampax down the toilet."

"I always tell her not to," Reiko said, "but she always does it."

"What the hell's the matter with her anyway?" I said, waxing up to a siege of frustrated hysteria. "We got little plastic bags for that kind of thing. Why doesn't she use them?"

"She does use them," Reiko patiently (I think) explained. "She puts little odds and ends of food she finds in the refrigerator in them—like a half a ham—to take home to her dog."

"Why doesn't she take home a few Tampax for her dog? The roughage might do him some good."

This discussion of Mrs. Gumpers took place a week after we had actually made some money from the hotel business. This had created a feeling of desolation in the village of Granby Lakes. Jesus! Everybody thought: If the Douglases make a success out of that goddamn hotel, we'll *all* be up the creek. This was one of the very good reasons why Mrs. Gumpers tried to flush insoluble objets d'femme down the toilet. Her cousin, Bart Gumpers, was the Granby Lakes plumber. Stopped-up

101

toilets were his specialty, he informed me one day over a warm beer at Jock Lee's bar, Granby Lakes' version of an English pub.

"E-yah," Bart Gumpers said, warming to his favorite and, albeit, his only conversational gig. "I've snaked open more toilets than anyone else in the state of Maine."

"Snaked?" I said, at the moment not being on to *that* term's connection with the opening of waterways with direct access to the nearest septic tank.

"E-yah," Bart Gumpers said, "you never seen a plumber's snake? Where you from, boy?"

"Well," I said, "I live up on the mountain. We just bought the hotel up there." Bart Gumpers started to laugh. Then he started to choke. Nobody in the bar paid any attention to this man, who, I thought, was going to need a quick tracheotomy with a dull can-opener at any moment. I presumed this happened all the time, or else the indifference in Jock Lee's bar had reached a high level. I presumed this after Bart Gumpers fell on the floor and turned purple-black. Jock, the bartender, who at the moment was rearranging the dirty sawdust on the barroom floor, just stepped over Bart Gumpers and asked me, in passing, whether he should pour *one* or *two* beers the next round? I said I'd let him know.

A few minutes later, Bart Gumpers, brushing the sawdust from his plaid mackinaw and adjusting his luminescent red hunting cap, was back at the bar asking the bartender where the hell his beer was?

Somehow I remembered our pre-choking conversation. "What's a plumber's snake?"

102

"Why don't you just wait and find out?" Bart Gumpers said. "Why spoil your evening?"

The connection between the ministrations of Mrs. Gumpers to our always ailing toilets and her cousin Bart Gumpers became quite apparent after his sixth house call. The toilets only became clogged after Mrs. Gumpers had serviced them, and Bart Gumpers was not needed until Mrs. Gumpers announced that there were cormorants in number three bathroom, diving for live eels.

"These two are working together," Reiko said. "When *we* flush, nothing happens, but when *Mrs. Gumpers* flushes, upstairs, it's raindrops falling on my head, from that stuffed moose in the living room."

"Maybe the moose has a cold," Bobby said.

"That's clever, Bobby," I said. "Whose side are you on anyway?"

"I'm on the side of the Lord," Bobby said.

"You're on the side of the Lord? Where did you get that?"

"Right here," Bobby said, "in the Billy Graham comic book."

"Now I've heard everything," I said.

"No, you haven't, Papa. They also got a Wonder Woman-Norman Vincent Peale comic book. WOW!"

"What do you mean—'WOW!'?"

"Well—"

"Well, what?"

"Well—Wonder Woman gets Norman Vincent Peale pregnant."

"And that's why they call her Wonder Woman, right?"

"Gee, Papa, how'd *you* know?"

103

"I've been writing those kind of jokes for years. Now let's forget about the funny stuff and get back to our gourmet toilets. What do you suppose Mrs. Gumpers will feed them today?" I said.

"I don't know," Reiko said, "I've hidden *everything* that could stop up a toilet."

"That may frustrate her completely," I said, "and next time she'll bring something of her own—like a used Volkswagen."

"That's silly," Reiko said, "a Volkswagen would never flush through a toilet!"

"With a little Vaseline, it would be a cinch," Bobby said.

Mrs. Gumpers was not the only chambermaid we had. They came and went like Bay of Fundy tide. (If any of you are unfamiliar with the Bay of Fundy tide and would like to know more, just look in the *Yellow Pages* under "Fundy Bay, Tides of.") All of our very transient chambermaids were related either by marriage or by blood to some sharpy artisan in Granby Lakes village, and all were equally skilled in creating in our guests (the few we had and kept) a feeling of "Oh, God! Where will it all end!!!?"

The first six months we were resident-owners of the Honeymoon Mountain Inn, and our guest toilets were under the benevolent care of the local orderlies of ordure, very little passed through our sewerage system, happily on its journey to our vast conglomeration of septic tanks. Everything stopped dead about halfway by a downeast Aswan Dam.

And all this because of the daily ministrations of: (1) Mary Ann Spunt. She was original in what she got the toilets to try and swallow. Besides the contents of the trash baskets, which usually contained razor blades, hairpins, Kleenex boxes, used-up tubes of Poly-Grip and Dentu-Creme, banana peels, peach and prune pits, hair, sox, half empty packs of Kools, full packs of Kools, little bags of poor-grade hash, and sweat-stained cross-your-belly bras, Mary-Ann tried other impedimenta, like a GI Joe doll and a Barbie doll locked in a position they both discovered while reading *The Joy of Sex* by Comfort. (I always thought a better title would have been *The Joy of Comfort* by Sex.) But nothing worked as well as a small bag of "ready-mix" concrete that alone immobilized our whole septic system for days. We had little cards printed for each guest room: OBSERVE NATIONAL PISS-IN-THE-LAKE-WEEK—SIGNED SMOKEY THE BEAR. This notice did very little to encourage this sort of outdoor activity and even less in building goodwill.

Kathy McCord was another of our quisling maids. Her husband was our Friendly Neighborhood Roto-Rooter man, which wasn't the greatest situation to be in—in a village where there was nothing to Roto-Root. Our hotel was the only place in town with indoor plumbing. Except Egil Grimshaw's secret system. He kept it a secret so it wouldn't be taxed. (In Maine they tax everything but your sperm, and they're thinking about taxing that, too, as soon as they get a way to assess it.)

Kathy McCord would throw nothing in the toilet bowls (we found this out later). She would just tear into our living room, screaming that if we didn't call the local Roto-Rooter man (we had no idea at the time he was her husband) that she couldn't be responsible for any tidal wave that might engulf our entire ground floor. This shook us up the first, second, and third times, but on the fourth time, when we saw this Roto-Rooter man grab Kathy McCord's left breast and her right buttock as he swung down from his truck, we knew right then and there that Roto-Rooter men were nothing but putty in the hands of any chambermaid who had a left breast and a right buttock. This and the enormous bills we got for this almost daily "service" made us suspect conspiracy, so, like a sneak, I drove down-country one evening and secretively bought a plumber's snake and brought it home. At midnight I quietly started snaking each guest toilet in turn. There was no obstruction at all, and this right after the day that Kathy had again reported that we needed another Roto-Rooter reaming. We didn't. We had been Roto-Reamed for the last time, so far as our plumbing was concerned.

15

THE only place in Granby Lakes village I felt wasn't too hostile toward our seeming ability to stave off disaster and keep the Honeymoon Mountain Inn alive, was Jock Lee's bar. You could not use the term "bar" in Maine, so Jock Lee's establishment, by law, had to be known as Jock Lee's Cocktail Lounge. When I asked Mr. Bidette (or a name that sounded like this)—the little snot from the capitol, as Reiko called him, and the field man or inspector or whatever from the Maine State Bureau of Alcoholic Beverages—why you could use the word "cocktail," but you couldn't say "bar," he explained, illogically, that "cocktail" did not necessarily mean anything alcoholic. It could mean a "shrimp" cocktail.

"In other words," I said, bristling slightly, "you reserve the right to sell a man a liquor license for five hundred dollars per year, but you also reserve the right to prohibit him from advertising the fact that he has liquor for sale."

"I wouldn't put it that way," Mr. Bidette snapped back. Mr. Bidette was a small odious man, and I felt that with very little encouragement, he could have been a nasty Allen Ludden. He used what authority he had (in the liquor commission) like a bull whip. He flicked it over the backs of all of us who had to cater to his tumid ego. To incur the displeasure of this pompous little honcho might get your "cocktail lounge" closed down for myriad violations. Most of the violations Mr. Bidette concocted on the spur of the moment, and by the time you could check up on him and clear yourself, months would go by. When the turd-who-walked-like-a-man—as Johnny Micmac, our local Indian, called him—finally signed a release reinstating you to the good graces of the Maine State Bureau of Alcoholic Beverages, you might be close to being very broke. So, Jock Lee, who was a real man, found himself groveling like an insecure debutante whenever Mr. Bidette slithered into Jock's place for a spot checkup.

"How *would* you put it, Mr. Bidette?" I said, not caring how he put it.

"We here in this state feel that alcohol should be controlled," Mr. Bidette said, using a tone, I felt, that he had cultivated just in case he was asked to speak at some high school graduation exercises. "Alcohol is a drug—"

"Hey, Jock," some local loudmouth at the other end of the bar shouted, "us junkies would like another round!"

Mr. Bidette ignored this, but I could see that he was making a mental note to remember that Jock Lee's bar was a gathering place for troublemakers, which may or may not be a violation. He then continued, "As I was saying, alcohol is a drug, and—"

"Then you mean that actually—when we buy that five hundred dollar license—we are actually buying a permit to peddle drugs. We're drug peddlers!"

"No. No. No." Mr. Bidette was sorry he had picked this unfortunate phrase, which he had filched from a

108

recent *TV Guide* in an article about Dick Van Dyke's being a closet alcoholic for eighteen years or however long. "What I meant was, we have to control the consumption of alcohol—"

"Yeah," I agreed readily, "especially around here—guess it's something to do with the climate—I mean, these long cold winters, what the hell else is there to do?"

"There's always humping," an enormous man, who smelled of sweat and Brut and more sweat, said, moving into Mr. Bidette's and my discussion. Mr. Bidette looked at the man, who must have been at least six feet eight, and almost as tall. He wore a stocking cap, a mackinaw, filthy blue jeans, and boots with sharp spikes, which were slowly but surely removing most of Jock Lee's barroom floor. Splinter by splinter.

"I beg your pardon," Mr. Bidette said, "but Mr. Douglas and I were having a private little talk here, and, well, I'm Charles Bidette from the Maine State Bureau of Alcoholic Beverages, and if I were you, I'd go home."

The giant thought this over, drank a bullshot in one gulp, then he turned to Mr. Bidette, picked him up by the seat of his baggy pants and his collar. Always the perfect gentleman, I held the door open for him as he carried Mr. Bidette out into Main Street and hung him by his belt onto a large hook, on the wall outside Jock Lee's bar, a hook that was formerly used to hang dead deer while the hunters went inside for a drink. Mr. Bidette started to scream and kick his heels against the side of the building, but the giant went back to the bar. Mr. Bidette screamed for me to lift him down; physically I couldn't have done it, but I didn't want Mr. Bidette to think that I was oblivious of his immediate problem,

109

so I told him that I couldn't help him down from the wall in front of the saloon because the Maine Alcoholic Beverage regulation, Page 265, Section 864, Paragraph B stated that any cocktail lounge with a sign or any other device that called attention to the presence of a place that sold alcoholic beverages was prohibited, and Mr. Bidette, by hanging by a hook on the outside wall of a saloon, violated this ordinance and should be reported to the Maine State Bureau of Alcoholic Beverages as soon as possible. I pointed this out to Mr. Bidette, precisely so there'd be no misunderstanding. I also explained that this was a Saturday night, and the Maine State Bureau of Alcoholic Beverages office did not open until nine A.M. on Monday morning. Mr. Bidette was frothing all over his neat blue serge and howling like a baboon with his balls caught in a venetian blind. I had to explain further to Mr. Bidette that he was hanging on the wall of somebody else's property, and if I were to interfere or alter the façade of Jock Lee's bar, he could sue me for vandalism, and I had no insurance against vandalism. Only buffalo stampedes. I then joined the giant at the bar. For hours as we talked we heard the varied tattoos of Mr. Bidette's heels against the outside wall of the cocktail lounge. These grew fainter and fainter as the giant and I drank more and more, and, I imagine, the heels of Mr. Bidette's Thom McAn hush puppies became worn down to his sox. Soxs don't make much noise.

That was just one evening at Jock Lee's. Jock was not particularly suited to the bartending profession. He wouldn't listen to anybody's sad tale of woe, the way a good bartender is supposed to do. If anybody would start, "My wife left me, today, Jock," Jock would look at

110

this bearer of domestic grievance long enough to make him uncomfortable, and then, when his dolorous customer was sufficiently cowed, he'd say, "Gonzales," and walk away. "Gonzales" is hard to answer unless you're drunk.

Jock had a very misanthropic attitude toward the world in general and his customers in particular. He was very annoyed if anyone dared to come into his bar, and he served them only as a last resort. If the prospective customer showed any signs of impatience at having to wait to be waited on, Jock would go to the men's room and smoke until the customer either left fuming, or calmed down and waited docilely for Jock to come back. But Jock Lee's was the only bar (cocktail lounge) in downtown Granby Lakes, and if you wanted a drink, you put up with a lot of crap to get it. And almost every drinker in town put up with a lot of Jock's special brand of crap.

Like every bar in the world, Jock Lee's had its collection of oddballs, weirdos, kooks, and practical jokers. Tucker Pyke had his pet mongoose, which he kept in a box marked DANGER—MONGOOSE—KEEP FINGERS AWAY— LAST RABIES SHOT July 27, 1968; inside the box was a large rat trap and a raccoon tail—somehow connected. Locally, this device was known as the drop-dead box because a few unwary summer visitors had done just that when Tucker invited them to take a look at the mongoose in the box. The summer visitor, mostly in desperation for want of something to do, would be very anxious to see the mongoose. Tucker instructed them to open the box and take a look—this was it; when the summer visitor opened the box, the rat trap would snap with a loud "Whapp!" and the raccoon tail would fly out, right into the face of the curious tourist, and he either survived the shock or he didn't. Tucker Pyke didn't care one way or the other, so long as the rest of the guys in the bar laughed. And they laughed every time.

There was a lot of laughing in Jock Lee's bar, but there was also a lot of arguing and a double-plethora of rough and tumble fighting. One January midnight a violent argument came to a head when two French Canadian lumberjacks disagreed about who was best with a thirty-six-inch chain saw. They settled the argument by charging out into Main Street, grabbing their chain saws from the back of their pickups, and before anybody could stop them, or cared to, they cut down twenty-three New England Telephone Company poles. In twenty-three minutes.

When questioned by "Fat Max" Collings, the village cop, the next day, Jock Lee said he didn't know anything about it; all he remembered was that there had been quite a wind the night before. That was good enough for "Fat Max," and he went back to his easy chair, his footstool, and Dirty Sally (not the TV show).

The chain-saw contest was well remembered until the next incident, which was presumably caused by the white lightning which Jock Lee served illegally after hours to a select few. This white lightning was nothing more than 180-proof vodka served in a full fourteen ounce Zombie glass, which had to be drunk with a straw. Those were the rules. Drinking almost anything alcoholic through a straw will give you vertigo, but with 180-proof vodka, anybody left after a bout with this kind of refreshment was called a survivor.

One bitter cold January night, during one of these illegal contests, a five-foot-four Irishman, whom no one had ever seen previously, suddenly proclaimed for all of Jock Lee's lushy customers to hear, "My name is Bernard O'Rourke, and I'm a general in the Irish Republican Army!"

There was no wild cheering after this rather unusual (for Jock Lee's) announcement. In fact, there was no reaction whatsoever, so the five-foot-four Irishman continued, "I'm a general in the Irish Republican Army, and I'm here to recruit recruits to join me on a march to capture Belfast from the dirty Protestants. Are there any dirty Protestants in this room?"

Unfortunately for the five-foot-four Irishman, there were nothing else but dirty Protestants in the room. And they were all six feet three. The five-foot-four Irishman started to speak what was to be his last speech of the evening. Before you could say Barry Fitzgerald or Jack O'Brian or Birch Bayh, the five-foot-four Irishman found himself out on Main Street where all the action in Granby Lakes on a Saturday night seemed to take place, hanging head-down from an old oak tree next to the town hall. There was something that disturbed him greatly, besides being hanged head-down from an old oak tree next to the town hall. Firewood—alder, maple, and pine—was being piled all around, neatly. Then he couldn't believe it, but he smelled the disturbing aroma of freshly spilled gasoline. Then, according to local gossip and Betsy Couzy, he told the intern at the Furbish County Memorial Hospital, the last thing he remembered was a loud "Poooooof!"

The intern nodded wisely, as he had been told to do at medical school, and went about the business of sewing the five-foot-four Irishman's ears back on. The intern had not been long out of medical school, and although he remembered to "nod wisely" as he had been told, he did not remember, the story goes, what he had been told about sewing ears back on—the *lobe* goes at the *bottom.*

But, as I think I said long ago at the beginning of this chapter, Jock Lee's bar was a haven for down-country people like me. As the Notre Dame Cathedral was for the Hunchback. I was safe here. The men and women of Granby Lakes who frequented this friendly oasis either grew mellow after a few drinks or else were on relief and food stamps and didn't need what the failure of the Honeymoon Mountain Inn could provide—like a new Skidoo or a twenty-five-inch color TV. These people didn't seem to give a damn that I was an outsider or had anything to do with any local operation or wore funny clothes (or what was funny clothes to anybody in Granby Lakes, like a hat that wasn't red or knitted).

After six months, or maybe a little more, the clientele of Jock Lee's bar accepted me or, at least, tolerated me as part of their loosely banded organization. It was an organized bunch, and one night I found out why. Jock Lee's bar was the secret gathering place for the Granby Lakes pariah group. Everyone who drank in Jock Lee's bar was number one on Egil Grimshaw's Enemies List. There was no number two or three, etc., on Egil Grimshaw's list; everybody, so far as he was concerned, was number one. They were the ones who either had come out losers in their dealings with Egil Grimshaw or, worse yet, winners.

I didn't know anything about this antipathy toward Egil Grimshaw or his iron grip on the village, until I mentioned one night that Egil Grimshaw was going to let me in on a development that he was planning for the south side of Granby Lake. This got a hoot from the assembled lushes.

"Let you *in* on it!" Mrs. Abernathy, Bobby's seventh-grade teacher, whooped, and sprayed the room with her Schaefer (she was having more than one). This signaled a group whoop and spray. No one could contain himself apparently.

When the first wave of mass hysteria had subsided, I asked what was so funny. This triggered the second wave of hooting and knee slapping. I suddenly felt as if I were back doing my monologue at the Blue Angel; only the Blue Angel crowd didn't whoop and holler or slap many knees—they just nodded appreciatively.

"Jesus, Douglas, you are really a pigeon," Mosher Parsonfield, the Granby Lakes undertaker, said. "First, Egil Grimshaw sells you a hotel that hasn't made a dime since 1912; then, in gratitude, you are going to invest money in one of his 'projects'!"

"His projects always make money," I said to defend myself.

"Yeah, sure they do, but not for the guys who are let in on the project; they always lose their asses while Grimshaw skims off the cream."

"How does he do that?" I wanted to know. "Doesn't he keep books?"

"And 'how," Mosher Parsonfield said, "three sets—one for you, one for the IRS, and one for him."

Again, everybody in the bar screamed with the hilarity of it all. Even Jock Lee, who disliked anything funny, managed to force out a chuckle, at the same time hating himself for it. All this lasted right up until the time there

115

was a sudden silence. Egil Grimshaw had just come in.

He was wearing a long black form-fitting overcoat, which made him look like a fat hearse. He flung his black lambskin hat onto a near peg, carefully hung his overcoat on the floor, and warped his belly like a cautious oil tanker captain through the narrow channel between the wall and a table and into a corner booth. Jock Lee took off for the men's room.

Egil Grimshaw waited patiently, sitting there behind his ponderous paunch with its sparkling jewelry lighting up the place. I couldn't help thinking, as I watched him, what a great background he would have made for the Sonny and Cher show.

Egil Grimshaw's patience never wavered, and neither did Jock Lee's. Finally, when it looked like a stand-off, Jock emerged from the men's room and took Egil Grimshaw's order for a double.

"Hey, Jack!" Egil had spotted me. *Lucky me!* Twenty-three people in the bar who hated his guts, and he singles me out to give a cheery "Hey, Jack" to. "Hey Jack! C'mere! Have a drink!" Egil was drunk. I could tell because it took him three tries before he got out the word "drink"—it was "drr-drrrr-drr-ink," like that very clever man on the Dean Martin show. Only Egil was for real.

Before Egil Grimshaw could bellow my good name once more and further instill the mistrust of my former drinking companions, I hurried over to Egil's booth and slid in next to him.

I had never seen Egil Grimshaw so drunk; usually he held his liquor and his counsel remarkably well, but tonight he was, in the parlance of the day, zonked. As soon as I joined him, Egil put his arm around my

116

shoulder and gave me a big Egil Grimshaw wink, which was less than a wink and more like he had been stabbed in the eye with a 2 x 4.

When Jock reluctantly slapped down Egil's double bourbon, Egil promptly knocked it over into his lap with his elbow, and said, "Jack, you're the sweetest guy who ever lived, and I just wet my pants."

"I hope," I said, "not on account of me."

"Hey, Jock, where's my drink?" Egil yelled, and the fuming Jock, who promptly brought him another double, this time made sure Egil closed his hand around the highball glass before he went back to wiping the bar.

"You know why you're the sweetest guy in the world?" Egil said, getting back to his theme.

"Not really," I said, and Egil knocked over his second untouched drink, this time into my lap. "And you just wet *my* pants."

"Not on account of me, I hope," Egil said. "Hey, Jocko, where's my drink? Make it a triple this time!"

Jock's face took on the look of a man whose hobby was disembowelment, but he braced himself and served Egil another drink; this time he stood by and waited until Egil got the drink to his lips before he left to continue wiping the bar—with a vigor that went down through seven layers of Dutch Boy bartop before he calmed his screaming nerves.

"Jack, you're the sweetest guy in the world," Egil said again.

"I thought that was already established," I said.

"Yeah," Egil said, "to think that you are going to put your little old five thousand dollars into my new project!" This was the first I had heard about my little old five thousand dollars leaving home, but being the sweetest guy in the world, I held my tongue (which was goddamn slippery).

Egil started to cry a little as he said, "Everybody else turned me down. All the lending institutions—Beneficial Finance just laughed at me, Household Finance just smiled, and Friendly Finance *spit*."

"They always spit," I said, trying to be sympathetic. "They're not in the loan business—they're in the spit business!" Egil Grimshaw didn't smile at this, so I had to.

"Five thousand dollars," Egil Grimshaw said, "you'll get back millions."

Everybody in the bar was listening now. Jock had stopped wiping, and also he had stopped serving. I wasn't really conscious of all this silence. I was too busy trying to think of a way to get *out* of this deal—where I'd make millions.

"You know what we're gonna do?" Egil said, and to a man, everybody in the room said, "What?"

"We're gonna build an oil refinery right here in Granby Lakes. Ari Onassis and me."

Again, everybody in the room Greek-chorused, "What?"

"Jesus Christ!" I said, in a way that could only have sounded like fighting words to a drunk. "An oil refinery in Granby Lakes? We're at least a hundred and fifty miles from the ocean. Where are we gonna get the oil to refine in this oil refinery. Drill for it?"

"You got it," Egil said, "you-hit-the-nail-right-on-the-head-how-about-another-drink-Jock-Jackie-*loves*-the-idea!"

Jock was startled into action, and everyone else start-

118

ed buzzing. An oil refinery in Granby Lakes—plus oil wells? Ari? Jackie?

"What," I said, to Egil, "what about the beautiful lakes and the mountains and the fish and the game and the trees and the pure clean air?"

"Fuck 'em!"

"Fuck 'em?"

"Yeah, fuck 'em!"

Then everyone in the room said, "Fuck 'em!" It sounded like a Holy Roller meeting with the hallelujahs coming in thick and fast. I thought they were all going to clap hands and stomp in unison next. And they did.

The next day I bumped into Egil Grimshaw in the Post Office and asked him when we could have a meeting about his oil refinery and drilling plans. He looked at me for a long time; then he said, "Gonzales," and left.

CHAPTER

16

AFTER buying three dozen of super stale Girl Scout cookies from little Betsy Couzy, I learned that the people of Granby Lakes village were getting damned impatient concerning our lack of failure. This all happened at the same time Reiko and I were getting impatient over our lack of success. Working our butts off just to break even wasn't what they had taught me at Vesco U.

"Success," Montesquieu, who must have been French, or maybe a guy named Levine, who wanted to bring a little more flair to his life, said, "success in most things depends on how long it takes to succeed." Then there was a guy who called himself Levine, because his real name was Montesquieu, who said that, "Success is like a glass of tea." Then he cleverly dropped dead before anyone could ask any questions.

I wanted more than anything else for the Honeymoon Mountain Inn to succeed. I knew that the right idea could do it, but the right idea eluded me until I discovered the existence, in thousands of full-page advertisements in millions of magazines, of something called the Club Mediterranée. It may even exist in real life. Whatever that is. According to the ads, the Club Mediterranée has thousands of grass shacks under thousands of palm trees all over the world. The copy in these Club

Mediterranée ads implies that the sexiest people in the world are members of this group, and then they show you a photograph of some of the members and spoil everything.

There are usually seven individuals in this suntan oil sautéed group, and they are *fat!* And with these seven fat people, you immediately get the impression that deep inside these seven fat people there are eighty-three tall, thin Watusis, screaming to get out and dance or, at least, to take a nice hot bath.

And all, male and female, dress in the skimpiest of swimsuits. The men wear what looks like the bottom half of Tiny Tim Pampers, and the women wear three Band-Aids that pass for bikinis.

This lack of female cover-up does not add to their appeal; their breasts, which are too small for tit men, are hardly worth covering, and the pelvic eyepatch that covers their most precious possession (if they're under sixty) only accentuates the unlovely bulge of their flaccid stomachs, making their navels look like a wary Cyclops peeking over a greasy hummock.

But this is not why I brought this fairly unalluring picture to mind. It's not why at all. The Club Mediterranée's member, because of his or her limited apparel, has no place to carry money. *Decently.* Money that they may need for booze at the beachside bar, the rental of a rubber surfboard, or a pay phone in St.-Tropez to call the little woman in Westport to tell her you're working late at the office. But this is no problem. The Club Mediterranée's sagacious managers have solved what might have been a deterrent to beachside fun by selling you, when you join this nonexclusive (judging from the ad photos) organization, *beads.* Beads that you wear around your neck like a lei, and each bead by its color denotes a denomination of money. For instance, a blue bead is worth a dollar; a pink bead, fifty cents; a yellow bead, twenty-five cents, etc. It is truly a wonderful gimmick and makes the spending of money much easier. As one member said, "What the hell—it's only beads." Which is exactly what the shrewdies who cooked up this idea wanted.

Nevertheless, whatever the Club Mediterranée may be, I liked the idea of using beads instead of money. I *still* liked the idea when Egil Grimshaw agreed with me that we should try it at the Honeymoon Mountain Inn.

Doubtful about this crazy new American scheme, Reiko asked, "But where will we get the beads? We have to have beads that nobody else has, or they'll be giving us counterfeit beads and we'll go broke."

"Don't worry about that," Egil Grimshaw reassured her, "just leave everything to Uncle Egil." He said "Uncle Egil" with a straight face, exhibiting more self-control than I've ever witnessed before.

We left everything to Uncle Egil because we wanted to restore a little of our faith in mankind. In spite of all the unbelievable stuff that mankind (such as it was in Granby Lakes) had pulled on us.

The beads idea worked out wonderfully well. Reiko, who still was the bartender, in self-defense against some of the local bandits who had mixed drinks for us previously, reported that the sale of booze had increased by more than five hundred percent over what it had been when we were accepting money instead of beads.

"We took in over a thousand beads tonight," she said the night we tried the Club Mediterranée method.

"What color?"

"Mostly blue—they're worth a dollar."

"I know, I know," I said, not with quite the enthusiasm Reiko enjoyed, but I felt pretty good about it. It seems that people will spend more of something that represents money—like beads—or scrip or somebody else's BankAmericard, than money itself.

After the first week, we took over eighty pounds of beads to "Uncle" Egil's bank, and when the first of the month rolled around and we got our statement, that's what we were credited with—eighty pounds of baby-blue beads. Money was never mentioned. Then—or *ever*.

CHAPTER

17

IN February of the first year of our unfortunate proprietorship of the Honeymoon Mountain Inn, it became quite apparent that the townsfolk campaign against us was succeeding. During the previous month we had taken in one dollar and fifty cents. This from a lonely ice fisherman who had wandered in on Saturday night (wearing hip boots) and ordered two warm beers (one for each boot). At the end of the month, as was required by the State Bureau of Taxation, we had to send them their five percent, which I had figured at seven and a half cents. I wrote a check for this amount and special-delivered it immediately. The State legislature debated for three days, then decided to accept it.

The other hotel-motels in the northern part of the state were knocking themselves out in bringing "live entertainment" to the eager public, to hypo their business. The eager public "didn't give a shit," old Mrs. Culligan (the chambermaid of the week) put it to us one day as she was striving, very successfully, to flush a toboggan and three stubborn rosy-cheeked little tykes down the guest toilet in the Warren G. Harding Presidential Suite and Lovenest. But we felt that we should offer the transient world something besides a bed and a Maine Continental breakfast (hot coffee and a bologna sandwich). I didn't know *what* until I read an item in Carrol Carrol's column in the weekly *Variety*, the show business Bible (they've given up the Gideon completely). Carrol's item concerned the huge profits hotel and motel owners were garnering via closed-circuit porno movies shown in the guest rooms.

I didn't know anyone who had a print of *Deep Throat* or *The Devil in Miss Jones*. I didn't even know anyone who had a print of *Some Like It Hot*, which I could advertise as a transvestite special.

If I may digress for a moment and drop in a little Hollywood ejectamenta—according to Sidney Skolsky, Marilyn Monroe, who appeared in *Some Like It Hot*, is still very much missed in Hollywood, and even now, ten years after her departure, Joe DiMaggio has fresh flowers placed on Arthur Miller every other day.

Actually I didn't want to show any porno movie at all—I just wanted to play a practical joke on the good folk of Granby Lakes. They wouldn't get the joke because their sense of humor was stillborn. On New Year's Eve we had advertised "A Gala New Year's Eve Party— All the champagne you can drink for $100," which I thought was mildly amusing, but the good folks of Granby Lakes took it seriously, if you can believe that, and didn't come near our party because they "couldn't afford the price."

The porno movie idea was along those same lines. I expected them to come from miles around lathered to the withers in lascivious anticipation. Then we'd show them something like Mary Poppins. Afterwards, if I was still alive, I would explain that it was just a practical joke.

Reiko thought this was living dangerously, but by this time I didn't give a good goddamn. I was sick of being frustrated, stymied, and thwarted by these bucolic bastards.

Finding a Mary Poppins-type film was not easy. I wrote to Hollywood. I wrote to London. I wrote to Rome and Yugoslavia. Nothing! I called Mary Poppins, but her number was no longer a working number. Finally, who should come to the rescue but the Father Damien of Granby Lakes—Egil Grimshaw. He dropped whatever philanthropy he was working on at the time ("Free Milk for the Dairy Lobby," I believe) and devoted the rest of the minute to my problem.

"You know Doc Philbin's Pool Parlor and Annie Green Springs Spa?" Egil said. I didn't, but I wanted to.

"It's behind the Granby Lakes Laundromat. You can't miss it. If you don't see it, you can hear it. Doc Philbin has gas." I thanked Egil Grimshaw for his kindness, wondering what he was getting out of it, and walked over to Doc Philbin's. Doc Philbin told me that he had an eight-millimeter print of *The Sound of Music,* which he would sell me for fifty dollars. Wary of anything that remotely resembled a "deal" in Granby Lakes, I moved with the caution of a nervous drunk riding a unicycle through a mine field.

"How come you have a print of *The Sound of Music?*" I asked Doc.

"An eight millimeter print of *The Sound of Music,*" Doc said, unsuccessfully suppressing a wine-flavored bell-ringer of an eructation.

"Never mind the punctuation," I said. "I never heard of an eight-millimeter print of a major movie."

"That's why it's worth every bit of fifty bucks."

"Who's in it?"

"Who's in *The Sound of Music*? You gotta be kidding. *Julie Andrews!* Who'd you think—Bette Midler? Janis Joplin? Maria Callas? Mason Reese?"

"Who?" I said.

"Forget it," Doc said. "You want this sixty-dollar film or dontcha?"

"Whatever happened to fifty dollars?"

"Inflation," Doc said. "While you were screwing around asking dumb questions—"

"Okay," I said, "here's sixty dollars."

"Just in the nick of time," Doc said. "Everything just went up another three percent."

"Horseshit," I said.

"That went up *five* percent," Doc said. "That is, if you can find any around."

I very much wanted to say that there never was, and never will be a shortage of that in Granby Lakes, but I didn't. I just sent him a Father's Day gift of a gross of mint-flavored, menthol suppositories, and they worked just fine. From that day to this he's never stopped jogging backwards into the wind. Whenever anybody asks him, "How are things, Doc?" he always says, "Cool, *real cool!*"

The first day of March fell on a Saturday and I felt this would be the night for *The Sound of Music* to be shown in the Honeymoon Mountain Inn cocktail lounge. I advertised it as an X-rated porno, both in the Granby Lakes Daily News and also with Charlie Ferguson and his loudspeaker car. I gave Charlie a couple of bucks extra so he'd say something nice about us and our entertainment that evening, rather than driving back and forth up and down Main Street bellowing, as he usually did, on his speaker that the Honeymoon Mountain Inn had cockroaches the size of coyotes—or whatever pleasantries he could think of to please the townspeople, and get us the hell off that mountain.

We had more than a hundred reservations for our midnight showing of our X-rated *Sound of Music*. We chose to show it at midnight because we wanted people to drink a little before the movie, and by ten o'clock we had several prone couples who insisted on doing the Freeport Frug on our tiny dance floor—horizontally.

When the old clock on the wall struck fifteen, which was as near as it ever got to twelve midnight, I doused the lights and started the film. The limit of our bar was fifty-three persons, according to the fire department, and we had never gone over that limit. Or even got close to it. But tonight was different. As the X-rated (by me) movie began, I counted fifty droolers and three slaverers who began licking their dirty chops in anticipation of good filthy film fun.

As soon as the opening bars of "The Hills Are Alive with the Sound of Music" came from my antiquated sound projector, they started groping each other. They were so engrossed in this foreplay to foreplay that they didn't hear the siren, and neither did I. The hint I had of anything unusual was the blade of an ax crashing halfway through the front door.

"What the hell!" I yelled, stopping the movie projector before broken-field running my way through and around the overheated customers to the door. "What's

128

going on?" I screamed like a wounded panther as I quickly estimated the damage done to the door.

"Open up before we crash the door down! It's the law!" an extremely rude voice answered from the outside.

"The door *is* open, you dumb bastard!" Charlie Ferguson said, his fingers releasing their talony grip on his wife's mossy dell. His wife seemed disappointed. Again.

The door opened and in strode "Fat Max" Collings. Fat Max was the local law, as I may have mentioned earlier, when he felt like it. Most of the time he spent at home watching television and drinking beer while his wife kept telling people who called about a murder that Fat Max was "out on a crime."

"What's goin' on here?" Fat Max seemed to want to know.

"We're showing a movie," I said. "Sit down and have a drink, and the next time you come, please leave your goddamn ax home!"

"Yeah," Reiko said, from nowhere, "we got enough trouble with drafts!"

"She's right," I agreed, in order to stall things a bit until I could guess at what this law-freak wanted. "We're thinking of changing the name from Honeymoon Mountain to Frozen Ass Hill—every time the wind changes, it—"

"Hold it," Fat Max said. "You showin' dirty movies here!" It wasn't a question. It was a loud statement. Fat Max was wearing a soiled (many times) raincoat and had a cigar butt in his left hand. In his right hand he carried a .45 Colt that must have been used by Wyatt Earp. He tried to spin it like Sammy Davis does, but he dropped it

129

and tripped the hammer. The gun went off, sounding like a sonic boom in those close quarters, and a bullet chipped a large chunk off the elongated penis of a tiki god we had brought from Tahiti some years before.

"My God!" Charlie Ferguson said. "Fat Max just circumcised Buddha!"

"I gotta arrest you and take you in," Fat Max said to me, as I wondered why Charlie Ferguson had thought that the Tahitian god belonged to the same club as Buddha.

"That's ridiculous," Reiko said. "Arrest Jack? For what? For being a Republican?"

"Are you kidding?" Charlie Ferguson's wife said. "A Republican couldn't get arrested in Maine. That's what Jack Anderson said."

"Jesus, Mable," Charlie Ferguson said disgustedly. "He said Rockefeller couldn't get arrested in Maine because if he did he'd buy it and give it to a friend! Jesus, Mable!" Charlie made for the bar with his empty glass. "Hey, Reiko, gimme another double!"

Reiko was busy trying to find out what the law-freak wanted and not finding out, so Charlie helped himself.

"I got a writ here," Fat Max said, "I got a writ that—"

"What's a writ?" someone wanted to know. Fat Max wasn't to be deterred by smart-ass questions. "I got a writ here—"

"Writ where?" Charlie Ferguson was back.

"Writ here—I got this right."

"Shouldn't that be," Mable asked, "right here, I got this writ?"

"Shut up, Mable, or I'll haveta run you in for interfering with legal procedures."

"Bullshit!"

"Who said that?" Fat Max beady-eyed the crowd.

"I did," Mable's sister, Gladys Upperly, said, spitting through the open portals of her beaverish front teeth.

"I'm gonna run you in, too, Gladys Upperly," Fat Max said, bulging his chicken breast where his silvery Granby Lakes Police badge stood out from his greasy mackintosh.

"Bullshit!" Charlie Ferguson said.

Fat Max stared long and what he thought was hard at Charlie Ferguson.

"Bullshit," Charlie said again.

"Just for that," Fat Max said, "I'm gonna run you all in!"

"That should be interesting," Moses Gumble said. Moses Gumble was Granby Lakes' *senior* senior citizen, and probably the only one in town who had finished grade school with an above C average. "How you gonna run us all in, Fat Max? You only got a little pickup truck with a little cage in it for stray dogs. Where you gonna put all of us? In there with the stray dogs?"

Fat Max decided that he'd better get back to the original scene. "This writ—and I also got a warrant—is to arrest Mr. Douglas here for showing a dirty movie in The Town of Granby Lakes. It's against the Granby Lakes' charter! And I got the charter right here!"

"The Granby Lakes charter was signed by King George the Three!" someone helpfully shouted from the back of the room.

"Yeah," I said, "lemme see the charter!" Fat Max didn't have much of a chance to protest as I snatched the charter from his sausage fingers.

"What's it say?" Reiko said.

"It doesn't say anything about dirty movies and it's

131

not signed by King George—it's signed by Egil Grim-shaw!"

"Holy Christ!" someone said. "Egil finally got George's job!"

Naturally, we didn't get into any trouble about showing a porno movie, even though half the town swears they saw the beginning of one, but we did get fined fifteen dollars for having one person too many in our cocktail lounge. Fifty-three was the limit, and we had fifty-four—if you counted Fat Max—which the judge did.

CHAPTER

18

THE day was breathtaking. It was that cold. The trickle of water that flowed from the hot water tap in our icebound kitchen meant the temperature outside must have been below zero. I looked at the thermometer. It was −32 degrees. We had, as the present fuel czar suggested, set our thermostat at 68 degrees. But try as it did all winter long the furnace just couldn't make it. A temperature of fifty-five degrees was the best it could do, which wasn't bad for a thirty-six-year-old furnace with emphysema. Reiko, Bobby, Timothy, and I crawled into the fireplace. We scorched our fronts while the ice age crept slowly up our backs. And this was in April.

I wanted to give Bobby and Timothy some brandy, but this wasn't Connecticut where kids routinely went directly from Pablum and Pampers to Courvoisier and Corvettes. I knew I didn't want to drink anything that might make me feel warm and forgiving. I wasn't against feeling warm, but I had to guard against any emotion that bordered on forgiveness or any form of amnesty for the Granby Lakes Plumbing and Heating Company (which knew nothing about either).

They had transformed our heating, with a few simple reroutings of pipe, into an impossible myth, with the result that our plumbing was frozen solid from October to May.

We were forced, when the need arose, to relieve ourselves into an empty plastic Humpty-Dumpty potato-chip pail, of which we had, at least, thousands.

If Humpty-Dumpty ever switched from plastic pails to another type of container, we'd eventually be in big trouble. I know from a frustrating camping trip experience—it's very hard to sit on a Baggie on a windy day.

We huddled closer and closer to the conflagration we had created in our fireplace, risking, but not caring about, the danger of incineration. A stranger peeking through a window might think we were warming up for a session of group suttee.

Bobby, our oldest and brightest, said, "Papa, have you got a fork?"

"You want a fork? Why?"

"I think I'm done."

We were *all* done, but it didn't matter. At −32 degrees below outside, and only a little bit above that inside, we could have practiced fire-walking and loved every minute of it.

"I wish I had some marshmallows," Bobby started again.

"Why?" I said in my role as straight man.

"I could stick 'em under my armpits and roast 'em," Bobby said.

"They'd only char," I said, because I knew—I'd tried it with chestnuts.

"I wanna live in Hawaii," Reiko said, in a voice filled with Oriental misery, which is probably the poignant kind. "Like I wanted to all my life."

"I wanna live in Tahiti," I said, "where I was born. I wanna go back to my little grass shack."

"Jack-san," Reiko said, with less misery and a lot more

134

impatience. "Why do always say you were born in Tahiti?"

"Because I was born on Staten Island, and what the hell does *that* do for anybody's sense of adventure and romance?"

"You want adventure and romance?" Reiko asked, discarding the misery and impatience and substituting amazement.

"Yes," I said, "just one more time."

"You certainly picked a helluva place for anything like that! Jesus! Granby Lakes, Maine! Why didn't we just move to the North Pole?"

"Yeah, Papa," Bobby agreed, "the North Pole's a great idea. Then, when we wanted to go south for the winter, all we'd have to do is take one step—in any direction."

I took a long hard look at Bobby, wondering if we could exchange him.

There was a knock on the door. It sounded as if someone were knocking on the door with an iron ball. The kind they use to knock good housing into a slum. The knock came again.

"I don't want to see anybody," Reiko said, "not until summer." The knock came again—bam! bam! bam!—rattling our framed nude photo of Chester A. Arthur's mother and knocking a few books off the shelves next to the door.

"I better see who it is," I said, "before the wall collapses. Jesus Christ! Who the hell is *that* anxious to see us around here?"

When I opened the door, six cubic feet of snow fell into the living room and I couldn't see anybody standing in front of me.

"Who is it?" Reiko asked.

"I don't see anybody. It must have been the wind."

"The wind doesn't knock," Reiko said. "It just comes in when it feels like it." Which was true, very true, at the Honeymoon Mountain Inn.

"I'm down here," a fragile voice said, "down here." And there she was—a tiny figure of a very frail little old lady in tennis shoes, bobby socks, and snowshoes.

"May I come in," she said, unstrapping her snow shoes and shaking out her flowered black satin hat.

"If you're from the Salvation Army," I said, "we'd like more hot soup and less singing."

"No," she said, brushing past me, "I'm Miss Harriet—Miss Harriet Quimpy—not Mizz—Miss."

"Oh," I said, feeling that that explained everything —with the exception of who the hell Miss Harriet Quimpy was and what the hell she was doing running around in subzero weather wearing white lace gloves, a dress that looked like an abused paisley shawl, and a flowered black satin hat.

"Would you like a cup of tea—I mean, to warm you up?"

"That would be nice," Miss Harriet Quimpy agreed. "Very nice."

"I'll make it," Reiko said, leaving her place at the fire with obvious reluctance.

"Oh," Miss Harriet said, seeing Reiko for the first time, "you're an Indian, aren't you? A Micmac Indian? Or maybe an Abnaki—or a Piscataqua. I'm very interested in the Indians and their problems."

"So's Marlon Brando," Bobby said.

"Is he an Indian?" Miss Harriet asked.

"I'm Japanese," Reiko said.

"Of course you are," Miss Harriet said, which left me completely nonplussed. Did Miss Harriet understand

136

Reiko or was this her way of being agreeable to anything?

"I'll get the tea," Reiko said, and she headed for our ice-bound kitchen.

"Now, Miss Harriet," I said, after slipping a low footstool under her sparrow ass, "what brings you out on such a day?"

"Isn't it glorious," Miss Harriet said. "It's like spring."

"Where?" I had to say.

"I saw a robin on my way over here," Miss Harriet said.

"You did?"

"Yes. I buried it. My, I love this old house. This was the old Sarah Selby House, you know."

"No," I said, not wishing to spoil her narration, "I didn't know. I thought it was always a hotel—the Granby Lakes Hotel."

"Oh, no," Miss Harriet said, a sad sweet smile wreathing her partially thawed lips. "This place has quite a history."

"So we found out," I said, "but not until after we *bought* it!"

"Then you've heard about the famous Sarah Selby? She was married to a sea captain, you know."

"Then one day," Bobby said, "he went to sea and never came back. Right?"

"Who is this darling child?" Miss Harriet said, patting Bobby on the head—buckling his knees.

"Oh, this is Bobby. He's twelve years old. And that's Timothy. He's five years old. He's the one lying there on the floor with the bottle and holding his ear—every time he has his bottle he holds his ear." I chuckled self-consciously.

Miss Harriet thought about this for a long moment,

then she said, "Don't you think he's old enough to—wean?"

"You mean from his bottle?"

"No, from his ear. If he keeps it up much longer, he's going to have one ear that looks like an ear and the other ear that looks like a wind sock."

"Here we are," Reiko said, as she set the tea tray and a plate with dainty little whatever-they-weres on a coffee table.

"You're very sweet," Miss Harriet said.

"I'm Japanese," Reiko said.

"Reiko," I said, before we got into the ethnic-distinction field, "Miss Harriet tells me that this used to be the old Sarah Selby House. Her husband was Captain Selby, a sea captain—"

"I know," Reiko said, "and one day he went to sea and never came back. Right?"

"Where'd you get that from?" I asked before Miss Harriet patted *her* on the head.

"On the late show last night. Errol Flynn and Lili Damita and Baby Le Roy. I think it was Lili Damita, or maybe it was what's-her-name? You know—Liza Minnelli's mother. Well, anyway—"

"Never mind," I said, and gulped a gulp of scalding tea, which warmed up my bronchial tubes so I could once again practice my new hobby, which seemed to be *coughing.*

"Sarah Selby—" Miss Harriet seemed to be settling herself for a long long looooong story, so I slipped a little Irish whiskey into my tea. "Sarah Selby," Miss Harriet started over, so we'd all get a grip on ourselves and really listen, "was my great-great-great-great-great-great grandmother."

138

"Gee," Bobby said, the first time I've seen him almost impressed by anything in a long time. "That was six greats."

"Supposed to be seven," Miss Harriet snapped, as Bobby moved away, avoiding another pat on the head. "Nevertheless, I have petitioned the government through some of our beloved Senators like Muskie, Fulbright, Javits, and Mondale to make this house—the old Sarah Selby House—a historic shrine. It's the oldest house in New England."

"That's wonderful," Reiko said, forgetting the cold and dampness for a moment. "Our hotel will be a shrine. My father will be very pleased about that. My father is a Buddhist priest!" This is true—Reiko's old man *is* a Buddhist priest, and every morning, noon, and night he's banging the drum slowly, the cymbals loudly, and the temple bells unmercifully, raising such a cacophony of reverence and screaming worship that Buddha does whatever he asks, just to shut him up. Makes you wonder if the Catholics are on the right track with just their little jingling bells. Maybe something louder would get people to shape up. It could cut down on so many confessions. And also save candles.

"No," Miss Harriet said, with more than a trace of impatience. "Not that kind of a shrine. This has nothing to do with religion; this has to do with history. History was made in this house. That's why I have asked the good Senators to get the government to condemn it—so they can take it over, and do what should have been done a long time ago."

Miss Harriet whipped out a sheaf of blue-ribboned legal-looking documents for us to sign.

139

CHAPTER

19

NEEDLESS to say (or is it?) we did not sign old Miss Harriet's impressive documents. I smelled a new Granby Lakes' trick in this latest maneuver, and also I had resolved never to sign anything again after our wrenching experience with the High Lama of Deviousness, Joseph F. Fulman. As Jock Lee, the bartender, once said, "Justice is blind, but when she's got Joe Fulman as a seeing-eye dog, she's really in trouble," which isn't the way Emerson would have put it, but it's not bad.

"Who is Harriet Quimpy?" I was bold enough to ask, a few nights later in Jock Lee's bar. I was bold enough because I was drunk enough. I was also stupid because I really did not want to know who Miss Harriet Quimpy was.

"Miss Harriet Quimpy is the village Little Old Lady— every village has one."

"Oh," I said, "well, she wants the Honeymoon Mountain Inn condemned."

"She does?" Jock said, his one eyebrow arched in surprise. (He had only one eyebrow, which went straight across his face, just above both eyes. And when he arched it, it disappeared into his hair, which wasn't much of a trip because Jock's forehead was in short supply.)

"You didn't know that?" I said. "You, the village bartender who hears everything, didn't know that Miss Harriet asked Senator Muskie and a whole lot of other U.S. Senators to have the place condemned?"

"No, I ain't heard nothin' like that," Jock said. "But what a helluva cute idea."

"What?"

"Funny, nobody ever thought of doing that before—not even Egil Grimshaw. We've had foreclosures, bankruptcies, liens, fires, floods, windstorms, and a few drop-deads, but 'condemned'—that's a *very cute idea!*"

"Jesus!" I said. "Whose side are you on?"

"Where you from? You a local boy?"

"No, I'm from Connecticut, but—" Jock looked at me for what seemed like an eon, then he said, slowly, relishing every oral morsel, "What—a—cute—idea!" I knew then what I'd suspected ever since we moved to the village of Granby Lakes—even in Jock Lee's bar I was in enemy territory, and nothing would ever change that, so I shifted gears a little and asked, "Why is Miss Harriet so interested in the Honeymoon Mountain Inn? She said something about making it into a historic shrine. What the hell does that mean?"

"Well, it's kind of a long story."

"Forget it then."

"It all started a long time ago, back when Squire Granby first came up here to Granby Lakes—'course, they wasn't called Granby Lakes then. But when Squire Granby came up to look over the land King George had given him, he thought it would be a nice place for a four-season resort—like it is now."

"Hold it," I said, "Granby Lakes is a four-season resort?"

141

"Do you wanna hear the story? If you don't, how about ordering another drink?" Jock said, snatching my empty glass and plunging it into something he called disinfectant solution, which was nothing more than dirty river water, which flowed out back of his saloon. I didn't want to offend Jock because, as unreliable and erratic as his ambivalence seemed to be, he was an important part of my spy system, which enabled us—some of the time—to keep ahead of the village saboteurs, who now seemed to have taken a sacred oath to see that the Honeymoon Mountain Inn closed just as soon as possible. Everybody in Granby Lakes was running low on cash. "Filthy" Phil, his local nickname, had pointed this out at the last secret town meeting, Betty Couzy, my other spy, had informed me.

I really didn't have to order another drink—Jock poured me one and continued his story. "Miss Harriet Quimpy's great-great-great-great-great-great grandmother was Sarah Selby."

"You left out one 'great,' " I said.

"Huh?" Jock said, losing his one eyebrow into his hair again.

"You only said six 'greats.' There are supposed to be seven." Jock Lee stared at me as if I had just stepped out of a flying saucer and had antennae instead of ears. No one had *ever* corrected him in his twenty-three years of barkeeping in Granby Lakes. He didn't realize it at the time, but he was aghast. He didn't know whether to hit me with the frozen pickerel he kept in the freezer to break up the Saturday-night fights or to have a double shot of rye. He had the double shot of rye, much to my relief, then he had a triple shot and continued: It seems that Sarah Selby was brought up to Granby Lakes by old

142

Squire Granby because, when old Squire Granby tried to sell off lots in the Granby Lakes' four-season area to people in Boston, nobody bought. Nobody came to look. Nobody gave a good goddamn about four-seasonal 50-x-100-foot building sites, two hundred and twenty-three miles from the Old Howard, and in those days a trip like that took eighteen weeks, if you were lucky and didn't get ravaged by a wino Indian or mugged by a renegade Pilgrim. I'd heard a similar version of this story from Old Miss Quimpy, but I didn't dare interrupt the hot-tempered Jock and his frozen pickerel.

Squire Granby got desperate and put an ad in the Boston *Globe*, "Free Land—For Godsakes!" This got some response, but not much. The first settler, who took title to three hundred and twenty acres on top of a small mountain overlooking Granby Lakes and the other beautiful mountains, was Sarah Selby.

Jock stopped his narrative long enough to gulp another triple. I thought he was going to continue, but he didn't, so having had four double martinis, I took over, extemporizing like a fool. "And Sarah Selby built a huge mansion on that small mountain and hired six girls from Hartford—or rather she lured six girls away from Prudential with promises of fabulous riches to be had in the mountains of northern Maine."

Jock's mouth dropped open. "I never heard *that* story!"

"I've been doing research," I said. *"Madam* Sarah Selby believed they would all become wealthy almost overnight because she knew there were many men in lumber camps who would give *anything* to have a woman. They would have given *anything* to have a *willing porcupine!"*

"I know the feeling," Jock said, "after looking at my

143

wife without her hair curlers." I must have looked puzzled. "She's bald," Jock explained. Then, shoving a bony finger into my chest, he said, "Go on." I took another slug and continued my wild fabrication, which, I knew down deep, I would regret later. "Sarah Selby had been almost right. There were men in the lumber camps who were starved for a little female contact, but there weren't as many lumber camps or men around, in those days, so Sarah Selby—to make ends meet—turned to real estate. She cut her three hundred and twenty acres up into 50-x-100-foot lots and put them up for sale. Foolish as this scheme had looked to Squire Granby, who had traveled this route some short years before, Sarah Selby sold quite a few lots—by taking low down payments and throwing in a girl with each lot."

"Gee!" Jock was fascinated by this mythical history I had cooked up. "Wait'll them Senators find out Old Miss Quimpy is conning them into getting the government to designate a whorehouse as a National Historic Shrine! Muskie may cry again."

"Maybe she doesn't know," I said, "or maybe she told the Senators the whole story and it appeals to them. Maybe it would be a coup—after all, what other nation in the whole United Nations has a National Historic Whorehouse Shrine????"

Jock's eyes narrowed and he reached for his frozen pickerel.

"You down-country son of a bitch—you're putting me on!"

"Don't be silly," I said. "*Think* about it!"

Whether they knew or not Harriet Quimpy heard from Senator Muskie and Senator Montoya the next day. They weren't in favor of condemning the Old Sarah Selby House (our Honeymoon Mountain Inn), but they weren't against it either. This so encouraged old Miss Quimpy that she immediately started around the state with a large petition and an oil drum (on the back of her pickup truck) to collect pennies from schoolchildren toward the purchase of this future historic shrine.

"I don't think you should have told anybody that the Honeymoon Mountain Inn used to be a—whorehouse," Reiko said. "They're liable to believe it, you know. Like the 'All the Champagne You Can Drink for $100' thing you pulled on New Year's Eve."

"I told about the whorehouse as a joke! That's all! Anyway, who cares what it used to be—that was years and years and years ago, and who knows, maybe it was a whorehouse!" I was beginning to believe my own lies. A good sign.

"Papa," Timothy said, "what's a whorehouse?"

"I'll tell you someday," I said, giving him a big love.

"I know what a whore is," Timothy persisted, "a whore is a prostitute."

"That's very good, Timothy," I said, "now go play airplanes with your brother." I gave him another big love.

"Papa?"

"Yeah?"

"What's a prostitute?"

20

BETSY Couzy sidled up to our table in the Yellow Apple, where Reiko, Bobby, Timothy, and I were trying to figure out what the Yellow Apple folks had put in our roast beef sandwiches. It looked like fat blotting paper, smeared with a mayonnaise that had been made with whatever was left after they mixed up a batch of STP.

Timothy dropped his sandwich on the floor and it clanked.

"Hya, folks," Betsy Couzy said out of the side of her mouth, an accomplishment she had acquired after watching TV prison movies. And X-rated eighteen-hour girdle commercials (which were only shown late at night on educational channels).

"You're still here?" Betsy said. "Nobody can understand it!"

"We don't want any Girl Scout cookies," Reiko said, and immediately Bobby and Timothy started screaming.

"Shut up!" I suggested to Timothy and Bobby, and grabbed two boxes of Girl Scout cookies out of Betsy Couzy's filthy little paws and corked up my darling children's mouths.

"You'll have to pay for those," Betsy Couzy said. "They're used—I can't sell 'em again."

"I'll pay for them," I said. "Now—what's the big spy story for today?"

"Well," Betsy said, flexing her lips back to normal, "nobody in Granby Lakes can figure out why you aren't broke. With everything that has happened to you."

"We *are* broke," Reiko said.

"You mean, you won't be buying any more Girl Scout cookies—I got to find another client?"

"Betsy," I said, "Reiko means we're almost broke, and I'll buy your cookies as long as you have 'information' for me."

She was relieved. "Supposin' I just make up stuff—just to sell my cookies—then what?"

"They'll find your head in a vacant lot. Your body will never be found."

"Jesus Christ! You play rough!"

"I have to," I said. "We're behind enemy lines."

"You can say that again," Betsy agreed. "They all hatecha!"

"How can they hate me? I *belong* to the *Garden Club!*"

"With them," Betsy said, "it's easy. My father says you are still a dum-dum."

"You told me that," I said, "and please inform your father that no matter what he says about me I'm never going to get my hair cut in your father's barber shop. I've seen his work. He's not a Maine barber—he's an Australian sheep shearer!"

"He'd still call you a dum-dum," Betsy continued, "even if he cut your hair every day. He says you're letting the town down."

"I'm sorry about that," I said, then to Reiko, "Honey, we've got to go broke faster. We're hurting the economy." Reiko didn't know what this meant.

147

"Well, I gotta get going," Betsy said. "Thank you for buying my Girl Scout cookies. You're contributing to a good cause."

After she was gone, I foolishly opened the second box of cookies. They exploded upon being exposed to the air.

"Come again," Mrs. Rogers, the proprietress of the Yellow Apple invited us, after I had paid for the sandwich facsimiles.

"Oh, we *will*," I said. "I'm thinking of throwing a royal banquet for Princess Ann and her husband when they arrive here for the fishing season. Do you think you could take care of that?"

"Oh, I'm sure we could—if you'd let me know what kind of sandwiches they'd like." I never found out whether Mrs. Rogers was putting me on or not. I think not, and I'm sorry I broke my rule—"never to joke with an idiot"—which sounds cruel, and I'm glad.

Driving up the hill to our Honeymoon Mountain Inn, I thought, perhaps for the hundredth time: Why amidst so much beauty and natural perfection, should there be such an undercurrent of perpetual dissatisfaction and ill will? Someone—or everyone—has said that no matter where you live there will always be problems, but I felt that Granby Lakes had far exceeded its fair quota.

"Mrs. Abernathy, Bobby's teacher, has started in on him again in school," Reiko said.

"How?"

"She told Bobby—in front of the class—that 'Douglas' is a French name and you know how they hate the French here in Maine."

"Douglas is a French name?" This was something I hadn't realized.

"Yep."

148

"Wait'll Douglas Fairbanks, Senior, hears about this."

"He's dead," Bobby said, happy to have a bad reason to join in the conversation.

"Then I'll tell him when I see him," I said. "Now do me a favor, Bobby—"

"*Anything*," Bobby said.

"Go give the animals some water," I said.

"Anything but that," Bobby said, but he changed his mind when he saw that I wasn't kidding.

After Bobby had left, I said, "You see what they're doing? They're trying to get to us—through our kids."

"You mean," Reiko said, " 'Douglas' isn't French?"

"No, it's Scottish and it means 'tender' and 'true.' "

Reiko couldn't believe this. "*You're* tender and *true!!!*"

"Lately, yes," I had to admit, "but never mind that. Mrs. Abernathy's cousin is Mr. Titterford—of the Titterford Hill Dairy."

"You mean the milk-dispenser burglar?"

"Yeah, and us not buying any milk from him at *his* price made him an enemy, and Mrs. Abernathy seems to resent this, and that's why she's giving it to Bobby in school."

"She shouldn't be allowed to teach school anyway," Reiko said. "She's a nutty old lady. That's what everybody in Granby Lakes says!"

"Yeah," Bobby said, rejoining us, "she's a fruitcake. She told everybody in the class yesterday that Mommie is Chinese."

"What?!" I said.

"I'm Japanese!" Reiko said, as if she had to clarify things.

"Mrs. Abernathy says that's the same thing," Bobby said.

"Well, you tell Mrs. Abernathy that she is full of shit," I, as the Father of the Year, advised his son.

"That's what I told her," Bobby said.

"My God! You'll be in the seventh grade for the rest of your life! She'll *never* let you go! She'll just keep you there and torture you *forever!*"

"Not forever," Bobby said, "I'll kill her."

"Now wait a minute—you can't go around killing people. It's against the law in Maine—unless you're deer hunting."

"It'll be worth it," Bobby said, "whatever they do to me."

I found out that he didn't tell Mrs. Abernathy that she was full of shit, but undoubtedly he thought it. She had been hounding him since he had entered the Granby Lakes Grammar School.

"Even in school," I said, "what a bunch of sons-abitches!"

"They sure are," Reiko agreed.

"Who?" Bobby said.

"Everybody," I said, as I had said before, "everybody but kids and dogs in Granby Lakes."

Each day seemed to bear out this misanthropic observation. The next vindictive action came in the form of a birthday party for one of the town's five-year-olds, to which Timothy, who was the same age, was invited. He came home and burst into tears. What had happened? All the other kids had been given cake and ice cream and a big balloon, but when it came Timothy's turn, they had just run out of cake and ice cream and big balloons.

I knew the moment I heard it that this was no casual oversight. This was a carefully planned spiteful act. I

150

held Timothy in my arms and hugged him and tried to make him forget this callous, insensitive cruelty. How anyone could hurt a little five-year-old boy was beyond my comprehension. But it had happened, and from that moment on Reiko and I switched from "Let's get *along* with the sonsabitches" to "Let's get *even!*"

CHAPTER

21

GETTING even with the birthday boy's mother, who withheld Timothy's cake, ice cream, and balloons, was a simple and very crude, but, I felt, necessary retaliation. I had Reiko, who was very good at candy-making, cook up a five-pound box of gift-wrapped peanut brittle, lovingly made with bite-size steel ball bearings instead of peanuts, which I sent to the birthday boy's mother, with a note: "To Mrs. Gertrude Hilstach, from An Admirer," which must have come as a thrilling pupenda-throbbing shock to a slob who had never had an admirer or anyone who had given her a second glance (including *Mr.* Hilstach) in all of her fat life.

The next time we spoke with Mrs. Gertrude Hilstach, we were happy to discover she still had teeth, although they seemed to flutter a lot on words ending in *s*.

This was only the first small step of ours toward the giant step we had planned for the mankind of Granby Lakes in the future. At the moment, we had to devote our energies to another problem with our Honeymoon Mountain Inn.

In running a hotel, even a small hotel such as ours, you must change the sheets every so often. I read this in *Anyone Can Make a Million in the Hotel-Motel Business* by my good friend Dr. Morton Shulman, a Toronto financial wizard. The good doctor had switched from his previously favorite subject, *Anyone Can Make a Million in the Stock Market,* for some reason. But to get on with it. You must not only change the sheets, but also replace them with clean ones, also clean pillowcases, bath towels, face towels, washcloths, and other miscellaneous.

I didn't have to read Dr. Shulman's book to learn this. We had been doing it right along until the day we were out—all day. And, as usual, after being away all day, we looked around when we got back to see if anything was awry. Everything was fine until we checked the laundry room. Somehow it looked a little empty. Probably because the enormous washing machine and the equally gargantuan dryer were gone. The spot where they had stood was bare except for a lot of severed copper arteries reaching up and out of the wall as if in piteous supplication. It was heartbreaking.

We learned later, from Betsy Couzy, who was better than any wiretap, that Mark Tolland and his suddenly nimble wife, Millie, had backed a Ryder Rental truck up to our laundry-room door and liberated our washing and drying equipment. They told someone they had forgotten to take them when they had moved out. We immediately started nailing down the fireplace, just in case they came back.

Without our own machinery we now had to depend on the Granby Lakes Laundromat. An appalling thought.

The Granby Lakes Laundromat was operated by a man with shifty eyes. Not the ordinary everyday, run-of-the-mill shifty eyes. Harper Fundy had shifty eyes that shifted in any and all directions, like gun turrets. He was fat and squat, and, with his eyes that swung up, down, around, sideways, and backwards, he looked like a heated toad. He also looked like a man who ran a crooked laundromat. And he was just that. The washing machines were wired to a secret button in Harper Fundy's change nook, and so were the dryers.

The Granby Lakes Laundromat is probably the only laundromat that has been rigged (by a former Las Vegas mechanic) so that if you don't get three cherries when you put in your quarter and pull the handle, you wind up with a large bagful of unwashed, undried, dirty stuff.

Not only are the washers and dryers tied in with Harper Fundy's control buttons, but they are computer-programed to break down at intermittent intervals, and always when Harper's not around, so no one can pin anything on him.

Putting a quarter in the Granby Lakes Laundromat washing machine was like playing a slot machine in Las Vegas. You know you have a chance to win, but you also know you could lose a lot of quarters before you do.

But either you used the laundromat or you beat your socks on a rock in the river. Which was a sure thing, but a lot less fun.

There was a hidden secret button connected with Harper Fundy's laundromat. Betsy Couzy told me this one night when she was clandestinely delivering four boxes of her stale Girl Scout cookies to me.

"The secret button," Betsy said, "is pressed by Egil Grimshaw. There's a hot line from the laundromat to Egil Grimshaw's office. When Egil Grimshaw presses that button, Harper Fundy puts all of the quarters he took in that day and leaves by a secret alley to Egil Grimshaw's office."

154

"You mean Egil Grimshaw owns the Granby Lakes —with the crooked machines—Laundromat!"

Betsy Couzy just winked.

After a few sessions at Harper Fundy's laundromat, we decided that not only were we losing the battle, but we were losing the war. No one could pay the laundry bill for the laundry we needed at the inn—even for the few people we had—so we dyed everything black. Sheets, pillowcases, towels, everything. If anyone asked about this unusual color, we told them there had been a garage sale at Buckingham Palace—right after Queen Victoria died.

Our tilt with the Granby Lakes rigged laundromat gave us another small opportunity to even the score with them and with the rest of Granby Lakes. We felt that six boxes of strawberry Jello in each machine allowed to harden would do it. It did.

For the rest of the summer everyone who had been surprised by this unexpected Jello envelopment had to *eat* his way to a change of underwear.

And Harper Fundy charged him extra for dessert.

CHAPTER
22

AT a town meeting on August 15 the people of Granby Lakes had just voted to impeach God. There was a good and logical reason for this. The Granby Lakes region had had sunshine for two days in a row, creating an influx of tourists and increasing our Honeymoon Mountain Inn business one hundred percent. Which sounds encouraging, but it really meant nothing because underneath the tinsel of these shining statistics were the rusty numbers of reality—from six guests, we had jumped to twelve. One hundred percent. Right?

Reiko and I were grateful for even this small bonus, but the Granby Lakers were not. They felt that a few more days of good weather and we'd break even. This was a catastrophe they didn't relish. God had given them the finger! Enough of a finger so that they felt they had grounds for impeachment. "Obstruction of Justice" they called it, which, of course, was the trendy thing to do.

God paid no attention to these troublemakers and let the Granby Lakes region suffer in the warm sunlight for three more days. There was another town meeting, during which there was some talk of hiring a plane to get up there and seed those clouds, but nothing came of this. They compromised and persuaded Dale Houle, the forest ranger, to use his plane, with its water scoop, for fighting forest fires—to scoop up a little water and dump it in the vicinity of our Honeymoon Mountain Inn. Which he did the very next morning. It was quite refreshing, and our twelve guests kept yelling for more, but Dale Houle, because of his nutty stunt, was deprived of his fire-fighting plane by his boss and reassigned to a twenty-five-gallon back tank and a leaky hose. This made Dale Houle think twice about ever doing anything again—that the town meeting suggested.

A Maine town meeting, I learned, was quite different from any other town meeting in New England, out of a perverse inclination to be *different*. The people in this region felt that everybody "down-country" was sub- or abnormal. Only *they* solved their problems the *right* way.

One of their problems was Egil Grimshaw, although no one would ever face up to it. Egil Grimshaw would generously donate a strip of his precious land to the village of Granby Lakes. The people at the Granby Lakes town meeting were always "overwhelmed" by Egil Grimshaw's unending "generosity." So far, he had given the town at least twenty miles of strips of his precious land. No one ever dared point out that these "gifts" were always strips that could easily be made into roads to be maintained by the town and that, by coincidence, they were always on direct routes to and through Egil Grimshaw's many housing developments.

The whole thing was so obvious to "strangers" such as we, but the villagers never protested. They kept their untidy mouths shut because they owed money to Egil Grimshaw's bank, and if they *didn't* owe money to Egil Grimshaw's bank, he had a way of suggesting that they buy a new car or a TV set or have a baby—this would bring them back into the fold at ten percent or more. Usually more.

The housing developments, which Egil Grimshaw had meticulously laid out in the hills around Granby Lakes, never really got going. After the "model" house was completed and sold, that was it. The model house remained the sole reminder that "Happy Acres," "Lakeview Acres," or "Pinetree Acres" was located in a planned community of one thousand half-acre plots —"with water, sewers, golf course, tennis courts, shopping centers, and recreation buildings soon."

Some of these incipient developments were twenty years old, and the first model home owners were still waiting with great anticipation for water you could get by just turning on a tap in the kitchen sink, instead of walking half a mile to the nearest creek, with an ox yoke and two eight-gallon buckets giving you a twice-daily hernia.

If someone demanded that some action be taken to fulfill Egil Grimshaw's promises, he would dispatch a backhoe immediately up to the complainer's area and start digging a long ditch. This satisfied the model home owner, and it took him weeks and sometimes months to realize that the backhoe had gone and the long ditch, now filled with greenish water, had become the breeding ground of millions of mosquitoes, who were so voracious that they were called Count Dracula groupies.

For a newcomer or a "down-country" upstart to attend a Granby Lakes town meeting was risky at best. Reiko and I found this out the first and only time we tried it. We were there to ask a few questions about our taxes, which were slightly higher than those on the Empire State Building. We wanted to find out why. And what our tax money was being used for.

At the grange hall where the town meetings were held, no one sat near us, which reminded me of my early years when I lived in a small town in California—the local movie house was segregated. The Indians sat on one side of the theater and the whites sat on the other. Actually this didn't help much. The Indians complained they could still smell the whites.

At our first Granby Lakes town meeting, we sat smiling and uncomplaining as would befit a newcomer. This didn't help. We were lepers at a symposium of squeaky-clean Christian Scientists.

Elmer Dipple, who was the chairman of the village's seven selectmen, seemed to be running things. "Miss Quimpy," he said, for openers, "will read the minutes of the last meeting." Miss Quimpy did just that, and the minutes of the last meeting meant very little to anybody. Miss Quimpy sounded as if she were reciting The Lord's Prayer in Yiddish.

The minutes of the last meeting disposed of, Mr. Dipple asked for new business. Egil Grimshaw stood up and proclaimed that he'd like to have some. Everybody laughed. Everybody who owed money to Mr. Grimshaw's bank.

Someone else, a frail but wiry old man, got up and suggested that the village of Granby Lakes accept a strip of land extending from Crow Point to Route 4 as a "town" road. The frail, wiry old man's speech sounded rehearsed, and it surely was because immediately, seemingly on cue, another frail, wiry old man got up (with difficulty, but spiritedly) and seconded the motion. Mr. Dipple said, "All those in favor, say 'Aye,' " and immediately slammed the top of the ancient table with a large gavel and continued, "Motion passed!" No one had a chance to say "Aye" or "Nay" or "Kiss my ass in Grant

City!" Just like that the motion was passed and became part of Granby Lakes law. Mr. Dipple glanced toward Egil Grimshaw and received a flicker of a wink in reply.

And so it happened that Granby Lakes received another burdensome gift of a road they had to grade and pave and maintain—and plow free of snow come winter.

Some crazy impulse made me stand up and ask, "Why is a road needed all the way from Route 4 to Crow Point?" This provoked more silence than I have never not heard before.

Finally, Egil Grimshaw said, "Jack, you don't know local conditions."

"Maybe so," I agreed, "but I've looked at every map of this region, plus the geodetic maps, and I can't see any reason Granby Lakes needs this road. Taxes are too high as it is. This will just add more tax."

"Only in certain cases," Egil Grimshaw agreed. "Only in certain cases." It sounded like a death sentence that he was pronouncing, and I didn't have to ask to whom he was referring, but I was in it now and I plowed on, tightening my own noose.

"What exactly," I asked, "do we get for our taxes now? Besides roads that go nowhere."

"You call Crow Point nowhere?" Egil Grimshaw was appalled.

"I would say so, yes. It's a little point of land sticking out into Granby Lake, and nobody lives there."

"But they *will* be living there." Egil was patient with me now, like Stalin used to be with some foolhardy wheat farmer who asked to be allowed to keep some of his wheat to maybe make some dinner rolls. "I visualize," Egil continued, "a thriving summer community out

160

at Crow Point, with water, sewers, a golf course, tennis courts, recreational buildings, a shopping center, and perhaps a massage parlor and a Kung Fu school." (These last were added for a laugh, which he dutifully received from his jubilant debtors.)

"Well," I said, not knowing then that I was bucking a real stonewaller, "if this whole thing is a big joke—"

"Not a *big* joke, Jack, just a little witticism to break up the monotony of these town meetings. Now"—Egil turned serious and seemed to have taken over the chairmanship from Elmer Dipple—"what about the budget? Does anybody have any suggestions?" If anybody had any suggestions, they didn't have a chance to mention them because Egil's next words were, "I move the Granby Lakes town meeting be adjourned. Anybody second the motion?" Again Elmer Dipple's gavel crashed down, and we found ourselves on the street.

"What was *that?*" Reiko wanted to know.

"Democracy," I said.

"What's 'democracy'?"

"I'm beginning to wonder, too," I said, leaving poor Reiko more confused than I was.

Before dawn the next day, bulldozers were cutting a road through virgin forest—from Route 4 to Crow Point. It seemed to me there was an awful lot of dynamiting—presumably of ledge and thousands or millions of tons of fill—across a large swampy area. But in three months the road to Crow Point was finished— not paved as yet—and Egil Grimshaw's real estate For Sale signs punctuated the landscape for miles around.

The whole procedure and its consequent events made me wonder about the official Maine state bird. Why did they choose the chickadee over the vulture?

After this August 15 Granby Lakes town meeting, our taxes were raised two hundred dollars. To offset this latest outrage, I felt that I needed help, so I contacted Norman, a writer friend of mine who had holed up for the summer in a tiny cabin high on Sugarback Mountain, to finish his latest off-off Broadway one-man sex comedy. I found him a willing accomplice when we met secretly one moonless night in the Granby Lakes village park. Three unknowing accomplices were the three Granby Lakes telephone operators who listened in on every conversation (of mine) as if they were being paid by a friendly foreign embassy.

"Jack?" a voice said. "It's Norman—I had to call. I don't want to alarm you, or anybody else in Granby Lakes, but I saw them again—just a few minutes ago—up on the ridge overlooking the village. There must be at least four or five hundred of them, and they are *enormous!*"

"Four or five hundred of them! My God!" I said. "How big are they?"

"Well, as near as I can figure—looking through my binoculars—at least eight feet or maybe ten feet tall!"

"Oh, my God!" I said. The connection was broken. And the stage was set.

CHAPTER

23

SOMEDAY I am going to write a key-to-success book along the lines of *How I Made Eight Million Dollars by Carefully Investing in My Grandfather Who Had Eight Million Dollars to Leave—When He Left,* or *Five Acres and Independence in the Mekong Delta,* or *How I Saved My Marriage by Raising Gerbils.*

My book will take the other side of the issue, the genesis being my own personal experiences, and I think it will be called *How Not to Ever Be Able to Retire—or Bad Investments Revisited,* complete with a seven-hundred-and-fifty-page cross-filed index.

To top off everything I've ever invested in before may be the Honeymoon Mountain Inn. *This* may be the high point of my business acumen. My keen insight of the direct route to the wide-open gates of bankruptcy. *I* didn't need a directional beam to help me find the key to failure. I did it all by a sharp sense of being able to bypass the minor dangers and get to the main pitfall in the shortest possible time. I was born a winner, but I fought it. Successfully.

The Honeymoon Mountain Inn—the good people of Granby Lakes thought, from outward appearances —was *not* on the verge of the collapse that was so necessary to *their* economic position. A sudden prosperous boom of ours would wipe out all of them. "They shall not succeed!" seemed to be their rallying cry, so it was at about this time that the real, unmistakable harassment began. It began subtly. As subtle as Granby Lakes could be. The telephone rang at 2:45 one Sunday morning. Reiko answered it. There wasn't much conversation on her part, and then after a moment she hung up and elbowed me awake.

"Jack-san, what's an orgy?"

At 2:45 A.M. this is a hard question to answer. Even at 2:45 in the afternoon it might still be difficult to explain what an orgy is to anyone who has never heard of an orgy. There are so many different types of orgies. It depends on what your pleasure is. An orgy to Alice Roosevelt Longworth or Margaret Chase Smith might mean an afternoon at a pet show. Then again I could be wrong about those two. An orgy to them might mean a weekend at the Happy Hours Motel with William O. Douglas and J. Paul Getty. Who knows? Maybe Art Buchwald.

Before I tried to explain to Reiko what an orgy is, I knew I would have to rely on fiction because in all my years in Hollywood I was never invited to one. For some reason I could just never get in with the wrong crowd. The telephone again—this time I answered it. A woman with an extremely spermy voice said, "Hello, Honeymoon Mountain Inn?" After I told her she had the right number and what could I do for her (I almost said "to" her), she said, "Have you got a room large enough for an orgy?" It must have been the same person who talked to Reiko, unless this was the Maine orgy season. I almost lost my head and got nasty, but my erotic curiosity got the upper hand. "How many in your party?" I asked, like the captain at Le Club d'Arrogance.

"Ten," Miss Sperm answered, "all girls."

"An orgy with just girls?" I was incredulous. And naïve.

"You got something against girls?" she said.

"No," I said, "and who is this? Don't you know what time it is?"

"We'll be right over," Miss Sperm said. "Wait for us." Then the phone went dead. After a while we realized, too slowly, that we had been *had*. I say, too slowly, because we *did* wait up, but, of course, no one showed and only the frogs outside our window were having an orgy. I could be wrong about that, too, because even when frogs are just sitting around thinking how rotten it is to be a frog, it sounds like they're having an orgy.

This post-midnight phone call was just the beginning. The beginning of many, many, many wild calls. It was the last call we got for an orgy, but we got many requests for reservations, which were unfulfilled. These cost us money. A Chinese dinner for sixty people who don't show up is mighty hard to get into the deep-freeze, and even harder to get out. A Chinese dinner for sixty people, unless wrapped with care, deep-freezes into one forty-eight-cubic-foot block of solid Fong Gon Ming Chow Hoong Shew Koo Lo Yuk. The next time we got a reservation for a Chinese dinner for sixty people we had to cut it up with a chain saw. We served it with chopsticks and a ball peen hammer.

Another favorite harassment, by the good folk of Granby Lakes, was the delivery of something we had not ordered. We were out for the evening. This happened upon arriving home at eleven, with two tired and cranky, impossible kids and a wife who, I felt, should try to be more like Shirley Jones and less like the Dragon Lady. We rounded the bend in our driveway, and there they were!!!! A three-story Winnebago DeLuxe Camper with a front porch and a built-in swimming pool (with a ten-foot diving board and a family of inflated swans). The camper was towing (or had been towing) a sixty-foot Chris-Craft Super-Cruiser, with a platform on the bowsprit for spearing skin-divers.

Reiko screamed, "We're gonna crash!" I slammed on the brakes, and all of us catapulted to the floor. Bobby was the first to recover. "Papa, somebody sent us a house!"

"Yeah, Papa," Timothy said, "and the *Queen Mary!*" A midshipman stepped out of the chart room and yelled "Ahoy!"

"Jesus Christ!" I said.

"No," he said, saluting smartly, "Captain Huffman at your service—and welcome aboard."

The roadside signs that were erected during the night and inspired by my tale of Madam Sarah Selby I'm sure were probably the most entertaining and harassing because they brought on a sudden influx of horny lumberjacks (and after three months cutting pulpwood back in the bush, their horniness was Olympian).

The sign I remember best and which caused a mile-long traffic jam to our door read HONEYMOON MOUNTAIN WHOREHOUSE. TONIGHT'S SPECIAL: BLOW-JOB 50¢—with Coolwhip, 75¢."

"Here's my fifty cents," a jolly green mackinawed giant said as I opened the door to his pounding. "Where's the broads?" I knew immediately what he meant because I had heard those very same words at some of Capone's two thousand cathouses in Chicago when Chicago was celebrating its first "Century of Progress."

"They're off tonight," I said, "it's a high holy day." As soon as I said this, I felt I had made a mistake—a high holy day to this French-Canadian bull would cut no ice. Catholics don't have high holy days. They have Lent and Bingo, Rykrisp and Ripple.

"Where are the broads?" the woodchopper repeated, his insistence swelling with his crotch. "Here's a buck—I'll take two."

"They have the clap."

"That's funny, so do I. Here's two bucks. Make it four—any color."

It took me a good half hour to put this frustrated woods-stud straight. I hated to do it and made a mental note—maybe "broads" would be a good idea. At least "broads," even at fifty cents a head, could help us pay the Granby Lakes property tax gouge.

By the time we had gotten rid of the jolly green prong, the cars on the highway and the drive up to the inn looked like a gas line during the shortage.

There were fistfights going on, evidently caused by some lumber jockey getting out of line and cutting in front of someone else. French-Canadian curses filled the gentle night air, and I thought I heard gunshots.

Reiko, who had been asleep at the time, wanted to know what the hell? Bobby and Timothy wanted to know the same thing. "I'm trying to sleep," Reiko said. "I thought you said Maine was quiet and peaceful?"

"It is," I said.

"Then what's all that noise and shouting and bang-bangs?"

"A bunch of pulp cutters. They want 'girls'!"

"Girls?" Bobby, who was growing up too fast, said, "Girls—for what?"

"Fifty cents."

"That's a lot of money," Bobby said, because his allowance was fifty cents a week.

"Yeah," Timothy said, "I only get a dollar."

"What?" Bobby screamed, outraged.

"You get *ten cents!*" I told Timothy, who, at age five, wasn't too hip about money.

"*You* couldn't get a girl then," Bobby said, practically and with satisfaction.

"You could get *one-fifth* of a girl," I told Timothy, as I could see the sibling rivalry bubbling up like a new volcano in a Mexican cornfield.

"Which fifth?" Timothy wanted to know, and I wanted to know how he knew girls came in fifths. Reiko wanted to know how to get rid of the howling mob that threatened to bulge our front door in, like the Big Bad Wolf in the Three Little Pigs, with his huffing and puffing. I knew there was only one thing we could do to turn back the tide of tumescent tree toppers, but it was the one thing that was not available, that is, not available in quantity—not in Granby Lakes at any rate. And quality was something entirely unfamiliar to these pent-up pulpers.

After three months back in the bush, Elsie the cow in a Fredricks of Hollywood negligee would have satisfied all but a sexual gourmet (who was also a vegetarian).

I got rid of our potential whorehouse customers by calling my friend, John, who was the local state trooper. He sized up the situation in a quick moment, then asked his wife if she would mind "streaking" past the line of cars and down the hill toward the frigid waters of Granby Lakes. From there, she was to make an abrupt left turn and streak back to the safety of her husband's prowl car. John's wife, who was a fun-loving girl from

168

Aroostook County and had been "Miss Maine Potato" before she was married, agreed to help out, and it worked just fine. For a while. Fifty or more wild woodsmen started as one, and they tore across the open fields in pursuit of this lovely naked woman who was only lovely in the unreliable eyes of these unfulfilled, so far, Children of Nature. Also, it was a moonless night. Cannon, the cop, would have looked desirable.

This got the wild bunch from away from our front-door step—and kept them away. The state trooper, who looked a lot like Sergeant Preston of the Yukon—he acted like him, too—was very proud that he thought of this ploy to lure the woodcutters down the hill into the icy waters of Granby Lake to cool their ardor at least temporarily. But he grew less proud and more anxious as the night wore on and Gladys didn't come back.

"Do you suppose they caught her?" he asked, his voice full of fearful wonder.

"If they did," I consoled him, "you'd better take off your gun and your Sam Browne belt and relax a spell"—local vernacular, I think. "It may be a week before she gets back. There were quite a few of them, and I doubt if once would be enough."

"Gee," he said, taking off his Sam Browne belt and his spurs (why he wore spurs in a souped-up Chevy only he knows), "I hope nothing's happened to her. Gladys has a cold, and, you know—the night air and all."

By this time Reiko and Bobby and Timothy had gone back to their little beds, and I was alone with Trooper John. "You don't seem very concerned," I said. "Your wife naked down there in the woods with sixty men."

"Sixty?" Trooper John stood up suddenly. "I thought you said fifty!"

This episode sounds very unlikely, in the retelling

and anywhere else in the country it would be, but in Northern Maine husbands were not plagued with possessiveness and crazy jealousies as they are in other localities. I thought this was a very adult attitude until I looked around again at the female population, and it was very easy to see why such inferior emotions—such as jealousy and possessiveness—never tortured their incipient minds. "To have and to hold" was something that applied only to fishing boats, snowmobiles, and hunting dogs.

The harassment by the locals continued on and on. And on!

Other signs, to zing us, were put up from time to time:

TODAY—FREE LUNCH AT HONEYMOON MOUNTAIN INN.
WELCOME PHILCO DEALERS AND BIG FOOT.

TONIGHT AT HONEYMOON MOUNTAIN INN—THE
ROLLING STONES! THE BEATLES REUNION! AND THE
ANDREWS SISTERS! SPECIAL ADDED ATTRACTION:
YOKO ONO!

This sign led to another near-riot. Hordes of people came from all over Maine, New Hampshire, and Vermont. Our very spacious lawns and the next-door golf course became an overnight dust bowl via the stomping of thousands of bare feet. We were at a loss and scared to death that these thousands would lynch us without benefit of effigy. They came to see The Rolling Stones, The Beatles, The Andrew Sisters, and Yoko Ono. We couldn't reproduce the first three, but we did give them a reasonable facsimile of Yoko Ono. We took a cocker spaniel, slanted its eyes a bit, dressed it in a muumuu, held it up to the window, and waved one paw at the crowd.

"Let's see your ass," some vulgarian yelled, which was no surprise because Yoko had shown her bare posterior on many an album cover. Whether this ever sold any albums I don't know, but it made her bared ass as recognizable as Martha Mitchell. This is not meant as an odious comparison.

Needless to say, *we* couldn't show this new howling mob Yoko Ono's well-flaunted buttocks, so in desperation we called the state trooper and asked if his wife was available for impersonations. He said, "What wife?" and that was that.

I had to go out on our front porch and explain to one hundred and fifty thousand barefooted music lovers there had been some mistake and the only entertainment we had were some cracked Lawrence Welk records and Timothy who was just learning how not to play the bugle. This satisfied no one, and they all took off for Boothbay Harbor where they marched into the sea like lemmings. Or, actually, better than lemmings because they were never replaced.

The episodes of harassment from the good people of Granby Lakes seemed endless to us and surprising —because we never knew what would happen next. These people had had many years of practice with the former unfortunate owners of the Honeymoon Mountain Inn, so nothing had to be planned. Almost every "dirty trick" was done by force of habit, like the night they chopped down the bathroom door. There was a good reason they chopped down the bathroom door, and the good reason was there was a fire in there and they were the Granby Lakes Volunteer Fire Department, and someone, Egil Grimshaw (?), had turned in the alarm.

Old Miss Quimpy, who had, sometime before, drunk a tall glass of prune juice, a quart of Haley's M-O, and swallowed three cherry bombs, was in the bathroom and did not rise when she saw the Granby Lakes Volunteer Fire Department surrounding her, as she sat wanly on the toilet. She had been sitting there for three hours when she was surprised by Fire Chief Burger and his men.

"Oh," Chief Burger said, "I thought you was on fire, lady."

"So did I for a while there," admitted Miss Quimpy.

"Sorry we had to bust your bathroom door," Chief Burger said to me, "but we can't stop to fool around and think when there is a fire in Granby Lakes. A lot of towns in Maine have disappeared overnight because of fire. We can't fool around—we gotta get the fire before it gets us."

"Yeah, I know," I said, "but what made you think there was a fire in our bathroom?"

"We got a call," he said. "Feller said, 'You better hurry on over to the Honeymoon Mountain Inn. They got a fire in their bathroom.'"

"Who called?" I foolishly asked.

"I dunno," Chief Burger said, "my old lady answered the phone, and her hearing-aid batteries ran outa juice a year ago. And you wanna know why I don't get her some fresh hearing-aid batteries?"

"No," I said.

"Boy! You're strange," he said and left, calling back

172

over his shoulder, "See you next week," which shook me up somewhat.

I called the insurance agent to tell him about the bathroom door.

"Was there a fire?" he asked, not at all with an Allstate-man manner.

"Well, no," I said, "you see—"

"No fire, no coverage," the insurance man advised, as Hitler would have advised Myron Cohen that from now on he would be doing his act for an all-Gestapo audience while hanging by his thumb (one).

"What about"—I managed some control—"what about my extended coverage?"

"That's only in case of a buffalo stampede," he said.

"Oh, I see." I forced a chuckle. "You're pulling my leg."

"Sorry," he said, "orthopedic work isn't covered either. The company may have to cancel your insurance."

"What the hell do you mean?" I said, without friendly pretense this time. "Cancel my insurance? Why?"

"Because the company is sick of your claims."

"But this is my *first claim.*"

"That's what I mean," he said, and hung up.

CHAPTER

24

WHEN Reiko, Bobby, Timothy, and I first arrived in Granby Lakes, we asked about a garbage man. We felt that was the one thing we could count on. Garbage. Time marched on—and on—and on—and on. Nothing happened. I looked in the Yellow Pages (mostly yellow from age), and the nearest I could get to "garbage man" was "GALVANIZING COMPOUNDS"—SEE "COATINGS, PROTECTIVE" and "GOATS"—SEE "PETS, NONPOISONOUS." Nothing in between. We had only one course open to us.

"How about a garbage man?" Reiko asked Egil Grimshaw. Egil Grimshaw was apparently caught off-guard—an unusual condition. Very unusual.

"A *what?*" he said.

"A garbage man, you know, someone to pick up the garbage."

Egil Grimshaw laughed. And laughed. His baked-bean-and-beer-filled belly was beating him to death. He enjoyed this immensely. "Someone to pick up your garbage?" And immediately he went into another paroxysm.

Jesus Christ! I thought. If this was all it took to make them laugh up here, I'd better set up a series of after-dinner speeches. If they pay enough, I'll be a riot. I'll be the down-east Will Rogers. Or I'll throw in a few quotes from the Bible, Aristotle, La Rochefoucauld, and *The Village Voice,* and I'll be northern New England's very own Senator Ervin. Or I can black up and be the Mount Washington Flip Wilson. And if I'm black, that in itself will be a novelty. Blacks are called exotics up here.

"What are we gonna do with our garbage?" Reiko insisted. "Save it—like the *National Geographic?*" Egil Grimshaw's quasi-Machiavellian mind started working, or maybe a better word would be "conspiring." I know it takes two to conspire, which worked out fine because Egil Grimshaw had Poseidon, his nonexistent partner, who had become an actuality in Egil Grimshaw's upbeat imagination. Right before our very eyes (I'm sure) Egil Grimshaw put together a new Granby Lakes Garbage Collection Company. "I have just the man for you—I mean, to collect your garbage—Filthy Phil."

"Filthy Phil," I said, still not believing that there was such a person. Egil Grimshaw was too quick and too alliterative about Filthy Phil. The name sounded like something else he had just formed, but I was wrong. Granby Lakes did have a Filthy Phil, a name he had been called ever since he built a little house on the bend of Route 4—just as the eager vacationer hit the Granby Lakes town line, which wasn't too far from the Granby Lakes business district. Truthfully, the town line and the business district were as one. Separated by a lonely pine tree and Filthy Phil's. The lonely pine was very sick from living too close to Filthy Phil's and the forestry department had sent for a Sierra Club priest to administer the last rites. The Sierra Club, of which I am a staunch

175

member, believed that no tree should die without being absolved of its sins. The lonely pine tree's only sin was living too close to Filthy Phil's.

At Egil Grimshaw's suggestion, Reiko and I and Bobby and Timothy called upon Filthy Phil at his Granby View Estates Home.

We couldn't believe it. Filthy Phil lived in a Pisa-leaning tarpaper and tin shack in the middle of five acres of abandoned cars, rusty refrigerators, three-wheeled hot rods, and no-wheeled baby carriages, bottomless aluminum canoes, overstuffed sofas with the stuffing bleeding from every Grand Rapids pore, tarnished brass headboards of long-since used brass beds—some of which held up the west wall of Filthy Phil's domicile. There was, at least, twenty tons of well-scattered jagged tin cans decorating the front lawn, or where there could have been a front lawn—which was an idea because Filthy Phil had at least eighteen or twenty bladeless lawn mowers accenting the field of rusted tin. The front porch of the place Filthy Phil called home was loaded with stuff he wanted to keep out of the rain. There were at least a half-dozen metal bread boxes, stacked high, their half-hinged doors engaged in endless suicidal wind-blown flagellation—to no avail. They could not die. Refrigerators with no doors at all formed an honor guard of chipped porcelain from the unpainted, loose-boarded front steps to the half-opened half-glass front door. There was a mat with the word WELCOME interwoven in rough coconut fiber. I knocked on the loose glass panel. A naked child soon appeared. Naked and dirty. So dirty that its gender was a matter of conjecture. Soon this harbinger of what was to come was soon

176

joined by three other children, each more dirty than the last. They were a study in advanced crud.

"Hello," I said in what I hoped passed as a friendly, carefree tone, "is Mr. Filthy home? I mean Mr. Phil. I mean your father, is he home?"

The children all looked at one another, apparently to see how the others would react, then dashed back into the house, slamming the glass-paneled door behind them. The glass-paneled door immediately developed a new set of glass cracks in its glass panel.

"Maybe we should go round to the back, to the service entrance," Reiko suggested. This from a little Japanese doll who had never heard of a service entrance until the night we went to a party at the Beverly Hills home of Norman Lear, a Hollywood tycoon who believed in the feudal system.

"Jesus," I said, "how the hell could anyone get to the back of this mess?"

"Hey, Papa! Papa!" Bobby began to shout. "Look—a dead cow." I couldn't believe it. There, lying in state among the empty pots and cans and defunct motorcycle parts, was a large dead animal. I took Bobby's word that it was a cow. I didn't want to know myself.

"What can I do for you?" The front door had opened silently, and there he was—Filthy Phil. I would have known him anywhere because his undershirt, which he wore out of courtesy to the flies, had not been washed since the day he had put it on, and that, I guessed, was sometime during the Coolidge era. His pants were more or less held up by one suspender, and many large horse blanket safety pins. His feet were bare and he had more than his share of toes.

177

"There's a dead cow in your front yard," Bobby said, and pointed.

Filthy Phil looked, as a courtesy, and said, patting Bobby on the head with a leprous paw, "You right smart, Sonny, right smart."

Bobby, who wasn't exactly an Ivory soap fan, backed off as though Filthy Phil were the Creature from the Black Lagoon, and, of course, we had no proof then that he wasn't.

"I," I started, "we want to ask you to come and pick up our garbage."

"Christ?" Filthy Phil said. "It can't be *that* heavy."

"No, no," I said, managing a polite, tolerant chuckle, "we want you to pick up our garbage every week and take it away."

"Take it away?"

"Yes."

"To where?"

"I dunno. There must be someplace to dump garbage around here."

"Oh, yeah, guess I still got some room—might have to shove that dead cow around a bit."

"How much will you charge us?" Reiko said, and with good reason. We had learned that, as with your physician, or your dentist, or your TV repairman, in Granby Lakes it's better to ask first because then the shock is lessened when you get the bill for twice the amount.

Filthy Phil gave this some thought, then he said almost brightly, "How about a dollar?" We could hardly believe what we had heard. No one in Granby Lakes had volunteered to do anything for a dollar. I thought there must be some mistake.

"A dollar?" I said faintly.

178

"Too much?" Filthy Phil said.

"No, no," Reiko jumped in quickly, "a dollar is fine. We'll see you when you come to pick up the garbage. Thank you very much." Then she hustled our little group back to our car, as Filthy Phil stood in the doorway squinting his eye at us. Then he waved "bye-bye," like a kid saying farewell to his grandmother boarding the Super-Chief for Barstow.

After three weeks we were wondering what had happened to Filthy Phil. He hadn't been around to pick up our garbage, and owing to a sudden influx of paying customers for our Chinese-Japanese and American dinners, we had fifteen twenty-gallon cans stuffed full, and the noise from the racoons prying the lids off every night was keeping us awake. The next morning we would spend until noon getting the Chinese-Japanese and American leftovers back into the cans from which the night creatures had spread them.

Finally, when the mountain of garbage was getting out of hand, I paid a friendly visit to Filthy Phil. He seemed to remember me.

"We haven't heard from you," I said.

"No," he agreed, "and I haven't heard from you. Where's my dollar?"

"You mean you want it in advance?" I said. "I never heard of paying for garbage collection in advance."

"Where you from?" Filthy Phil wanted to know. "You a local boy?"

"No."

"Oh, then that's why."

"Why what?"

179

"Why you never heard of paying for garbage collection in advance. Up here it's cash on the barrel head."

"My God," I said, "why didn't you tell me?"

"You didn't ask. If you were a local boy, you would have asked."

"Okay," I said, "but you haven't been up to collect the garbage in three weeks. Here's your dollar."

"Three dollars," Filthy Phil said.

"What?"

"Three weeks, three dollars."

"Okay," I said, trying not to sigh too loudly. "Here's your three dollars. When will you be up?"

"First thing," Filthy Phil said, "first thing."

I thought about asking whether "first thing" meant the first thing in the morning or the first thing after the twenty-first century, but I decided against it. Why give my ulcer an ulcer?

The next day Reiko and I and Timothy spent all of our time, almost, in sitting next to the back window hoping to get a glance at Filthy Phil's truck coughing up our winding driveway. We might just as well have spent the day waiting for the second coming of Sonny Tufts. Filthy Phil did not come to pick up our garbage.

I called Egil Grimshaw and asked him, as a village father, would he please ask Filthy Phil to perform his part of the bargain. Egil Grimshaw said he would get right on it, and he did, and sure enough two weeks later, Filthy Phil showed up with his 1934 pickup truck, which had solid tires. By this time our garbage collection had reached twenty-seven overflowing cans.

"Well, let me see now." Filthy Phil pulled out a ragged notebook and a well-chewed pencil and started to do a little cyphering. I didn't know, but I had a feeling about what he was doing with that pencil and notebook. He kept counting the number of garbage cans (which had cost us a mild fortune to buy), then writing these figures down in his notebook.

"I make it twenty-seven cans," he said after what seemed like an hour of calculus, algebra, and the old math. "That'll be twenty-seven dollars, plus tax."

"I thought you said a dollar."

"For one can. You didn't tell me you were gonna have this kind of garbage. This is no small-time operation. This is volume, man—vol-*ume!*"

He hyphenated words he wanted to emphasize. And annoy.

"Where were you when we had only three cans?" I said, as if it made any difference.

"I can't keep rushing up here every time you got a little garbage. I got a business to run!"

I was becoming disquieted by this time, or else I wouldn't have asked. "*What* business?"

"I'm a selectman," he said. "I vote on how much property tax you pay." If ever I heard a veiled threat, this was *it.* But I felt that sooner or later we would have to take a firmer stand about everything in Granby Lakes, so I took up the flung-down gauntlet and asked him, "You mean, if I don't give you one dollar a can to pick up our garbage, you are going to vote my property tax higher? Is that what you mean?" There must have been something about my revised tone or my demeanor because Filthy Phil edged his way toward his pickup truck. "Something like that," he said.

"Fuck off!" I screamed, and Filthy Phil, in one fluid

181

motion, was in his pickup and barreling down the hill toward safety and, I imagine, to Egil Grimshaw's field headquarters.

I should not have been rude, or I should have been rude, but more suave. While effective, "Fuck off!" shows a weakness in vocabulary and forethought. But it certainly worked, and maybe the word—or these two words—would spread throughout the length and breadth of Granby Lakes and maybe, just *maybe,* some would think that the Douglases were not quite the sitting pigeons they were thought to be.

From that day forward, we dumped our garbage in a little gully in back of Thomas E. Yates' property, causing him to spend most of the summer wondering why his lovely six-country-acre estate suddenly began to smell like Jersey City.

Betsy Couzy had told me that Thomas E. Yates had *always* looked like he was smelling something, and now he looked like he had *found* it.

Filthy Phil, for his lack of concern about our garbage and his not-so-veiled threat about our taxes, put him at the top of our "Get-Even-with-the-Sonsabitches List," but what to do to retaliate was a problem that would take a little thought. A bath, we were sure, would be the supreme revenge if we found some way to give him one, but, upon careful consideration, we decided this might not be the smartest thing to do. A bath might kill him.

I finally came up with something less violent, but more enduring. They were having a sale on Elmer's Glue down to Greens Corners, and I bought out their entire supply, then one day when Filthy Phil and his

182

family were away, I spent the better part of an after-noon gluing his firewood together. All eight cords of it. It cost a small fortune for enough Elmer's Glue, but it was worth it. Filthy Phil wouldn't even know about it until winter, then I thought Reiko, Bobby, Timothy, and I could all sit in our nice warm car on a nice forty-degrees-below day and watch Filthy Phil go rapidly and freezingly crazy trying to solve his woodpile.

Later, just at dusk, I got another prearranged phone call from my friend, Norman, from his lair high up on Sugarback.

"Jack, it's Norman. I saw them again—"

"Oh, no!" I said, my voice fearful.

"Oh, yes, and they're *much bigger* than I thought! And there are a lot *more* of them than I thought."

"This is awful!" I said. "What are we going to *do?*"

"I don't know," Norman said, "but I think they're getting very restless and—"

The phone went dead.

CHAPTER

25

THERE was some reaction in the village *this time* to Norman's mysterious phone call. Several groups of people were standing around in the lobby of the Granby Lakes post office, whispering (as I came in).

After I had opened my box and received my full quota of junk mail and threats from the Granby Lakes Power Company, I tried to smile at everyone at the same time as I made for the door.

"*What's* up in the mountains?" Miss Hinkley, Egil Grimshaw's girl friday and part-time inamorata (according to Granby Lakes gossip) asked, on the verge of tears, as, it seemed, always.

"What mountains?"

"The only mountains we have," Miss Hinkley said, one lone tear caught on the edge of her left eye. "That phone call you got last night—Alma the operator said—" She stopped because she knew she had said a little too much. "We heard," Miss Hinkley bravely continued, "everybody in the village knows there's something up there in those mountains that—"

"Gee," I said, "Miss Hinkley, I wish I could help you out, but I don't know anything, and I didn't talk to anybody on the phone last night. I never talk on the phone on Tuesdays. It's this sect I belong to and—" I let it go at that and walked out onto Main Street. Now I was *really* a stranger to mistrust. Not only was I from out of state, but I *knew* something and I wouldn't tell *them*.

Reiko and I, with our Honeymoon Mountain Inn, weren't the only ones in Granby Lakes to get "ripped off." Egil Grimshaw, the Florence Nightingale of the flimflammers, spread his benevolence in other profitable directions when the occasion warranted it.

The Beachside movie theater had been purchased about the same time that we had bought the hotel, by Gurlain Partridge, who happened not to be a native son of Granby Lakes and who had made a good thing out of his project. The Beachside theater was located in a former garage, but it had five hundred uncomfortable seats and a screen that could almost accommodate widescreen films.

Actually, the Beachside theater's screen could only accommodate one-third of a wide-screen film. The other two-thirds ran over the edges of the proscenium and up and onto the two side walls of the theater, which were decorated in early Goodyear. Old tires, chains, fan belts, headlights, auto horns that worked by squeezing, and many other automotive supplies from the golden age of Bluebook-Greenbook travel hung there, so that when a wide-screen movie like *Gone with the Wind* was being shown, a lot of the action took place on the two cluttered walls and was very hard to make out. The burning of Atlanta looked like a luau in a Hawaiian junkyard.

Egil Grimshaw, who (naturally) had sold Gurlain the

Beachside theater, became restive. Gurlain was making too much money, and Egil, who was cursing himself for not demanding a percentage of the take when he had the chance, felt that it was time for a change of Beachside owners. So he suggested to Gurlain that he winterize the theater so that it could run all year, and Gurlain would become wealthy overnight or, at most, in one year.

Gurlain Partridge, who was nobody's fool, he thought, pondered this suggestion. The Beachside theater was packed all summer—from July 4 to Labor Day—and with movies that cost him next to nothing in rentals. Movies like *London After Dark,* starring Ben Lyon and Bebe Daniels. *The Return of Frankenstein's Bride,* with Mary Miles Minter and Spade Cooley (an early Western TV star). *The Return of Frankenstein's Bride's Mother-in-Law,* starring Elmo and Abe Lincoln (not the martyr) and Carmel Myers, a lovely young thing who formerly had made Rudolph Valentino, who was playing Tarzan, cream in his Klopman loincloth.

It was hard to believe, but these ancient and dreadful movies played to packed houses. Night after night. Because there was nothing else to do in Granby Lakes after the sun went down. Nothing that was listed in the Chamber of Commerce bulletin anyway.

After meditating for almost a day and between phone calls from Egil Grimshaw—urging him to make up his mind—Gurlain Partridge thought the winterization of the Beachside theater was a great idea. Especially after Egil Grimshaw assured him, a hundred times, the poor people who *had* to stay in Granby Lakes all winter didn't have a goddamn thing to do except to avoid home-canned botulism and watch television.

Gurlain Partridge spent the entire month of Septem-

186

ber (after Labor Day) hammering thick sheets of insulation anywhere he could hammer it and shove it. He also spent all of his capital on a new double roof and a heating system, sold to him by Egil Grimshaw's brother, Vergull Grimshaw, who just happened to be starting a heating business that September.

Gurlain was so happy with his newly winterized theater—he turned the heat up full blast one hot September night and just sat down in the theater all alone, and enjoyed the magnificent sensation of warmth in what had been a drafty garage ever since it was built in 1912. It wasn't until Gurlain noticed that his nose was beginning to smoke that he turned off the heat and went to bed, to dream of the riches that would be his any winter now.

Funny—it didn't turn out that way. Gurlain Partridge opened the winter season on a Monday night with a magnificent movie, *The Sex Fiend of Wimpole Street,* but everybody in Granby Lakes stayed home and watched *Maude.*

Tuesday he had *White Christmas* with Sammy Davis Junior. Everybody in Granby Lakes stayed home and watched Jack Lord, of *Hawaii Five-O,* trying to solve a pineapple.

Wednesday, Gurlain gave them a Walt Disney, *Charlie the Lonesome Voyeur.* Everybody in Granby Lakes stayed home and watched *That's My Mama.*

Gurlain was getting desperate by Thursday. He tried to get *Deep Throat* and *The Devil in Miss Jones* as a double feature, but he had to settle for an Italian Western called *Rock Hudson Takes a Hot Bath and Finds Himself,* but everybody in Granby Lakes stayed home and watched *Ironside, The Streets of San Francisco* and Walter Cronkite telling them that's the way it is.

Friday had to be big, Gurlain reasoned, so he let down a little and showed them a repeat of Tony Curtis and Sidney Poitier handcuffed together and loving every minute of it. This meant nothing. Everyone in Granby Lakes stayed home and watched the *Seven Million Dollar Man,* which used to be the *Six Million Dollar Man,* but the price had been adjusted because of the added cost of fossil fuel.

Saturday night was Saturday night, Gurlain reasoned—they *had* to go out, so he showed four full-length porno movies and seven Donald Duck cartoons, plus free popcorn and contraceptives for couples in the balcony.

All for naught. Everybody in Granby Lakes stayed home and watched Mary Tyler Moore, and everybody's favorite zombie, David Carradine, kicking the balls of every stunt man in Hollywood, on Kung Fu. After that, anybody with any sense got drunk, got into a fight, and got into bed. And another fight.

Sunday, Gurlain Partridge left town—and the theater keys with Egil Grimshaw. Monday, the Beachside theater became a garage, until July 4 of the following year, when the Egil Grimshaw theater presented *London After Dark* with Ben Lyon and Bebe Daniels. To a packed house.

CHAPTER

26

WE had great difficulty in classifying the Granby Lakes villagers, that is, separating the swindlers from the incompetents, although, in all fairness, most of them were both.

Reiko and I debated whether to have our faithful old car ministered to in Strunkville, which was a good fifty miles away, or have it done here, where it was handy, in Granby Lakes. We felt that to have your car repaired or even tuned up in Granby Lakes is like having Evel Knievel teach your five-year-old child how to ride his tricycle. It's risky. The only garage in town is owned by Elmer Dipple, and he calls it the biggest garage in downtown Granby Lakes, which is a pretty safe statement since it's the only garage in downtown Granby Lakes.

Our 1960 Land Rover (which we had used back in the bush in Canada) had run out of windshield wipers, and up here, where you must have your car inspected every six months, windshield wipers are *de rigueur* (which is French for windshield wipers, our new French-Canadian maid of all-play-and-no-work told me). I took the Rover to Elmer Dipple's garage and left it with complete instructions about what needed to be done. Three weeks later I received a call from Mr. Dipple himself, which right away told me we were in trouble.

"About your windshield wipers," Mr. Dipple began, "both motors are burned out."

"What does that mean?"

"New motors."

"Okay," I agreed, because I had no choice. "When can you have it ready?"

"What month is this?" Dipple wanted to know.

"It's October."

"How about November, toward the last?" Mr. Dipple asked and hung up.

I didn't even get a chance to answer or agree, but again his was the only game in town and that was that.

Much to my surprise I got a call from Mr. Dipple on December 17. "Car's ready," he said and hung up. He must have been the number-one quick-hang-up champ of all New England, I thought as I made my way through a light snowstorm toward Dipple's garage. I walked because I needed the exercise, and I enjoyed it very much. The "light snowstorm" would have been considered to be a crippling blizzard anywhere except in northern Maine, but much to my surprise I found Dipple's garage through the driving snow.

Mr. Dipple gave me a bill and backed off quickly. It seemed that the motors for Land Rover windshield wipers were just about the same price as motors for a Lear jet, but what could I do—windshield wipers need motors and it's the law. After thanking Mr. Dipple for his kind and prompt service, I wandered around the service yard until I found my car. By some miracle it started right up, and I tore out of the driveway before the storm could get any worse. On the highway back to the Honeymoon Mountain Inn, I switched on the windshield wipers. Nothing happened. The motors, which, on a Land Rover, are mounted in front of you just above the dashboard, were working just fine—clicking back and forth as they were supposed to. But the thick snow was piling up on the windshield, and I could see nothing.

Rather than run the risk of slamming head-on into a truck carrying two thousand tons of pulp wood, I stopped and got out to see what was wrong. So far as I could see there was only one thing wrong—there were no windshield wipers. All that was there were two little squared steel stumps wiggling back and forth, wiping nothing.

The wipers themselves had been removed and not replaced, either by carelessness or design. I preferred to believe the latter, and added Elmer Dipple's name to our rapidly growing shit-list.

It took quite some time to think of an ingenious way to give Elmer Dipple the shaft, but eventually I learned that Elmer Dipple had a reputation for having the most terrible temper in Granby Lakes. This gave me my opportunity.

The chief target for his explosiveness, outside of his wife and family, was his bulldozer (he was one of Egil Grimshaw's road builders).

The bulldozer in question was the most enormous thing I have ever seen. It must have weighed at least fifty tons and it could flatten a whole range of hills in an afternoon, when it was working right. But, on cold mornings, Elmer Dipple had the very devil of a time getting it started. This is when he would boil into a rage, become an instant maniac, and run inside of his house to get his old Army Colt .45. Returning, he would start shooting wildly at the bulldozer. This violent action had no effect on the bulldozer, but it cooled Elmer Dipple down to his old sour self.

This nutty habit of Elmer's gave me an idea, one cold early morning in October. The leaves had already changed color and fallen dead off the birches, aspens, and whatever, and the weather was very brisk, so I knew Elmer would have trouble starting his monstrous machine.

Just a little before Elmer came bounding out of the house to get on with the day's work, I secreted myself in a group of thick cedars, right in back of the bulldozer, weighted down with two heavy revolvers.

I didn't have long to wait before Elmer came out of his house. He wasn't bounding this morning. He was just shuffling, as if he knew he'd have no luck with the giant bulldozer. And he was right. After a few sustained tries, nothing happened. Elmer jumped down from the bulldozer cab and started to scream wild, howling epithets at the machine and then dashed back into the house. He came out almost immediately with his old Army Colt, a moment after I had crept into the cab. Elmer was white with fury as he pumped nine slugs into the inert monster. Then, panting and spent, he stood and stared at the object of his frenzy.

In the darkened cab, after a count of five, I stuck my revolvers through two holes in the heavy metal cowling and blazed away all around him. This violent reaction from his hitherto submissive bulldozer sent Elmer Dipple into a wild panic. He shrieked and threw himself to the ground and stayed there, squirming, his hands alternately protecting his head and his crotch. A splendid example of indecision.

192

From that day forward, Elmer Dipple was known as the village liar. Nobody *ever* believed his story.

At dusk the phone call came.

"Jack? . . . It's Norman."

"I know."

"Again today."

"You saw them?"

"I'm looking at them right now through my binoculars. They seem closer than before. Closer to the village."

"Maybe we should warn everybody. These giant creatures may be dangerous!" My voice was filled with anxiety.

"No," Norman said, "nobody would believe it, coming from an out-of-stater, and maybe—just maybe—they'll go away and nothing will happen. Oh, my God!"

"What is it?! What happened?!"

"They just tore down the old mill! Two of them ripped it up into thousands of tiny pieces. They just *wiped* it off the face of the earth! I've never *seen* such—"

The phone went dead.

LATER, when dusk had given way to a lovely full-mooned night, the telephone rang again. It was Eldon Moult, the Granby Lakes town manager. A town manager in New England is much like a mayor in the outside world. It's his job to see that the snowplow is not working. Whatever else he does has never been explained.

"What can I do for you, Mr. Moult?" I said.

"Well, Mr. Douglas"—he seemed nervous—"I've been seeing some strange—er—creatures, up in the mountains." Mr. Moult, apparently, was on a fishing expedition.

"Oh?" I said helpfully.

"Er—yes," Mr. Moult said. "From my office window."

Mr. Moult's office was up above the post office and had no windows.

"Oh?" I said again. Not so helpfully this time. I didn't say anything further. I found out long ago that when you are speaking with someone on the telephone, if *you* don't talk, the other person will feel obligated to fill in the embarrassing silences. Mr. Moult felt this obligation strongly, since our conversation seemed to be going nowhere. And downhill.

"We've been talking at the Town Office about your re-quest to lower your property taxes, "Mr. Moult said, re-vealing his desperation.

"Oh?"

"Yes, now what about those strange creatures up in the mountains you've been told about? What are they? Maybe moose? Or?"

"Gee, Mr. Moult," I said, "I don't know what you're talking about."

"You don't, huh?" Mr. Moult's tone had changed con-siderably, and not in the direction of congeniality.

"You must have the wrong party."

"No," Mr. Moult said, "I have the *right* party, and about your *property taxes*—"

I hung up.

"Maybe we'd just better quit and move out," Reiko said at supper (supper in New England is dinner in the civilized world). "They hate us!" Reiko was starting to boil a little.

"Wait a minute," I said. "I don't think they hate us be-cause we are us. I think they hate us because they want to resell the hotel and they can start in again by redoing everything they have done before. It's the only way they can survive. They've got to keep this thing a failure, and the most times they can get this place to revert from one owner to another, the better."

"Egil Grimshaw is a *p-r-i-c-k*," Timothy said, which made us very proud. It was the first word he ever spelled.

"It's not only Egil Grimshaw," Reiko said. She was close to tears now. "It's everybody. How can they be so cruel?" Seeing Reiko in this condition ended any empty

195

defense I had always put up about the attitude and methods of the Granby Lakes residents to sink our little ship and get rid of us.

"Timothy's right," I said. I was cold as ice now. "Not only about Egil Grimshaw, but about every one of those rotten bastards out there!"

That night, lying in bed, with the moon making fantastically beautiful shimmering shadow effects up and down the lake, which spread endlessly before us from high atop Honeymoon Mountain, my thoughts weren't directed toward anything that was beautiful and good and unspoiled. I felt only the sharp jabbing shafts of unrequited revenge. In the half-world between awake and sleep, I tried to think of some way to make them sorry they had ever done what they had done to us.

They had hurt me, but what was more important was the damage they had done to my beloved little Reiko and my two precious children. I could *not* forgive this. They had hurt *me* by systematically wiping out most of my life's savings. If my family were suddenly left without me, there would be nothing for them.

The greatest liability in my life is my inability to take anyone or anything seriously. I have always felt that life is ridiculous. Fun, but ridiculous. This chink in my psychic armor has been my undoing at many a serious meeting of writers, producers, and other determined humans. Inversely, this personality quirk has kept me going through a lot of soul-searing moments. And now, despite my intense desire on the surface, at least, for retaliation against the Granby Lakers, my plans for revenge bordered on the hysterically ridiculous. I wanted to create a crazy, wild, and even hilarious form of retribution. I kept half-dreaming of the alternatives, the best of which seemed to be (in my semicomatose state) a dance contest for all the Granby Lakers in a hall with a quicksand floor. And just as everybody in Granby Lakes was about to disappear forever into the quivering mass, screaming for me to save them—very deliberately I'd uncoil and throw them a *long rope,* which just happened to be an *anaconda* (that hadn't eaten for months).

Just before I dropped off, Norman called. "I didn't see them today. Maybe they're gone." Then he hung up.

CHAPTER

28

AT seven A.M. the telephone again, and a voice I did not recognize:

"Do you think they're *really* gone?" the voice asked.

"Who is this?"

"Never mind! Do you think they're really *gone?*"

I hung up. The phone rang every few minutes all morning long, but we didn't answer it.

"What do you think they'll try to do to us next?" Reiko asked later, on our way back from our weekly trip "down to Rumford" to pick up our quota of Humpty Dumpty potato chips and six one-hundred-pound bags of fresh cow manure.

"What *can* they do?" I said, immediately thinking of hundreds of things they could do that they hadn't done so far.

"What are you gonna do with six hundred pounds of fresh cow manure, Papa?" Bobby asked.

"Never mind," I said.

"It's secret cow manure," Timothy said.

As we drove up the blind curve in our driveway, we almost ran into the back of Filthy Phil the garbage man's 1934 pickup truck.

"What the hell is he doing here?" Bobby asked.

"Maybe he's changed his mind about our garbage and wants to make a deal," I said, but I doubted it.

Filthy Phil was nowhere to be seen until we got inside the house. There, in the living room, in my chair, his feet on my hassock and drinking my beer in front of a roaring fire, was Filthy Phil—with a few more layers of grime than when we last saw him. His dirty undershirt was covered by a dirtier undershirt.

The shock was too much, and I forgot my perfect host role, which actually I had forgotten years ago. "What the hell do you think you're doing? And get the hell out of that chair!"

"I smell something funny," Timothy contributed at just the right moment.

"Ain't this the old Sarah Selby Mansion?" Filthy Phil wanted to know, in what I felt to be a decidedly disrespectful tone. He then flicked a cigar ash on our twenty-dollar-per-yard new carpeting.

"Bobby," I said, "go get my rifle."

"Which one?" Bobby said. "The .22 or the Colt AR-15 automatic with the twenty-round clip?" I thought Bobby was laying it on a little thick, but "yeah, that's the one," I said. Filthy Phil ignored us completely.

"How's your dead cow?" Timothy wanted to know. Filthy Phil dropped another load of White Owl ash on our new carpet.

"What is he doing in our house?" Reiko said. Reiko was extremely sensitive to the occupancy by anyone but our family of our living room. She had never read *The Territorial Imperative,* but she had the deep, passionate, and inborn ferocity of a wild creature when it came to protecting her own domain.

"I don't know what he's doing in our house," I said. "Bobby's up getting my rifle." Filthy Phil added a few more ashes to the rapidly mounting pile on the carpet. Bobby handed me the rifle. I pulled back the cocking device and let it go with a loud clicking thunk. The rifle (which had no safety catch and a hair trigger) was ready to fire. I was carried away by the melodrama of the thing and pointed the rifle at Filthy Phil. Filthy Phil put two fingers into his mouth and whistled a shrill ear-splitting whistle. Immediately the four naked kids we had seen at his garbage-heap home appeared, along with his female creature wife, and a young slatternly daughter who was dressed like Daisy Mae.

"You want us, Pop?" the Daisy Mae asked.

"Yeah," Filthy Phil answered. "I need you for witnesses. This man here"—referring to me—"is gonna shoot your father."

"Oh, wow!" was the Daisy Mae's reaction. And that's all.

"What's he gonna shoot you for, Paw?" The wife wanted to know.

"Wants us to leave his house."

"We ain't gonna leave this house," the Daisy Mae said. I thought the joke—the obvious put-on by some warped Granby Lakes village mind had cooked up as just one more harassment—had gone just about as far as I wanted to go. I tried to remember how Humphrey Bogart would have used a rifle to prod someone with, but I came up empty, so I just held the AR-15 with the twenty-round clip next to Filthy Phil's dandrufferous head. This was an extremely stupid and dangerous thing to do because if the rifle had accidentally squeezed off a

Remington .55 grain hollow point bullet, Filthy Phil's head would have immediately become a shambles. I felt it was also my turn to speak. "Who says you ain't gonna leave this house?"

"This does," Filthy Phil said, pulling a ragged but importantly legal-looking document from somewhere deep in his dirty underwear. Reiko took the document and held it for me to read. It seemed to be some sort of court order, and it contained the name "Philip Selby."

"Who's Philip Selby?" Reiko asked.

"Who else," Filthy Phil said, and his entire family burst into raucous laughter.

"You?" I said.

"You know," Timothy said to one of Filthy Phil's children, "we got a skunk family that lives under the house. Maybe *that's*—"

"Never mind!" I said, trying to pat Timothy, but succeeding only in raising a nice bump on his head with the swinging butt end of my rifle. Timothy cried right on cue.

"You mean"—Reiko was not to be deflected—"you are some relative of Sarah Selby, the madam who once owned this place?"

"Yep, the old Sarah Selby Mansion has been handed down from generation to generation until it finally got to me—Philip Selby."

"This is a crock of shit," I said. "Now come on, get the hell outa here or I'll call a cop."

"Jesus!" Filthy Phil said. "You gonna wait for 'Fat Max' to show up, you got a long wait. 'Fat Max'—he don't make house calls." I knew Filthy Phil was right about this.

"Look," Filthy Phil said, "why don't we all just simmer down. This is *our* home now, and we ain't leaving. We're staying *right here!*" With this, his mildewed family made themselves comfortable all over our living room, while the youngest of the naked children suddenly and thoroughly relieved himself in the nearest corner. Reiko grabbed the rifle away from me.

We had the good sense not to consult Joseph F. Fulman, the lawyer who had handled everything so well for us when we had bought the Honeymoon Mountain Inn. We found another man, who did not seem to be tied in with any of the local schemers, and he told us that somehow it had been discovered that—through, mayhaps, a new long-lost will or whatever—that Filthy Phil Selby *did* have a claim on our property.

"Fine," I said, "then Mr. Tolland, the man who sold us the property, did not own it either, and it wasn't his to sell. And also Mr. Grimshaw, who sold it to Tolland, after his bank had foreclosed on someone else before that did not have a right to sell it to Tolland, and so on—far down the line to the original owner, Sarah Selby. Right?"

"Something like that," Emil LaBoute, our new lawyer agreed, "but it's very complicated."

"Do you think we can get our money back? And all the money we've spent trying to improve the place and so on?"

"Well," Mr. LaBoute said, "it's *very* complicated." Which implied some ray of hope, but certainly not very much.

"You know what?" Timothy said to the lawyer, LaBoute.

"What?" LaBoute asked Timothy, and he seemed genuinely interested.

"That skunk family we had living under our house— they moved out."

Norman hadn't called for three days.

CHAPTER

29

"YOU know what you ought to do?" Jock Lee said to me, as he poured very little bourbon into one of his optical-illusion shot glasses, the same kind of shot glasses they used in some of the ragtaggle bars on Chicago's North Side. The glasses were constructed so that you could not get your little finger into one, but the glass was so faceted that it looked as if you were getting a very generous one and a half ounces of Kentucky Gatorade. I had shown absolutely no interest in Jock Lee's leading remark, so he regrouped his brain and his lips and repeated it, "You know what you should do, Jack." I couldn't help starting to listen. I thought that, by some miracle, Jock might have a solution to our problem of Filthy Phil's moving into our Honeymoon Mountain Inn. So I said, "What should I do?"

"You should write a book about Granby Lakes."

"Oh, my God!" I said. "Who'd *believe* it? And *why* should I write a book about Granby Lakes?"

"Because, well, for one thing, nobody has ever written a book about Granby Lakes, except a few people."

"What did these 'few people' who wrote books about Granby Lakes say about Granby Lakes?"

"Well," Jock said, "they just said how nice it was up

here, with the mountains and the lakes and the fall foliage and stuff like that."

"Gee," I said, like Andy Hardy just discovering that Ann Rutherford was a girl. "Gee, that sounds real intter-*est*-ting and exciting—a book about *fall foliage* and stuff like *that!* I bet it would sell better than *Black Beauty.*" Jock Lee's eyebrow disappeared into his low-growing hair. He was puzzled by the mention of *Black Beauty.* It couldn't have been anything else.

"*Black Beauty,*" I said, "it's a book about this beautiful black girl—you know, like Diahann Carroll or Teresa Graves. She falls in love with this man, but she can't marry him."

"Why not?" Jock said, lowering his eyebrow into its accustomed groove. "Why can't she marry him? I know! Because she's black and he's white?"

"No," I said. "It's because she's black, and *he's* black. That kinda stuff doesn't work anymore. You ever see a black football player with a black girl *lately?*"

Jock was puzzled and so was I. I got taken off by a flight of fancy that led nowhere. I quickly changed the subject, but not quickly enough.

"What the hell are you tryna do?" Jock was mad. "You think you down-country wise-asses can come up here and pull the wool over our eyes?" This was an unfortunate choice of phrase because Jock's hair was like a merino sheep's and it grew down over his forehead, and when he frowned a little, he couldn't see a thing.

"Chrissakes!" I said, not wanting to encourage the outraged Jock into playing the "Washington Post March" on my head with the frozen pickerel he kept ready behind the bar. "I'm just giving you my opinion, that's all. Don't you think that a man has a right to his opinion?"

"Not in *my* bar," Jock said, tightening his overhand grip on his frozen pickerel.

"Okay," I said soothingly, trying to calm things down. "What were you saying? I mean, about what I should do—instead of cutting my wrists and lying down in the bathtub with one of Solzhenitsyn's three-laughs-on-every-page novels?"

Jock felt for his frozen pickerel again, then changed his mind. "Oh, I think you should write a book about Granby Lakes."

"Oh, yeah." I knew I had to agree.

"You should talk to old lady Granby."

"You mean—of the Granby family? Still here in Granby Lakes?"

"Sure, once they settle here, they just don't move away. They *like* it here!" This sounded like another challenge, so I immediately agreed that there was no other place *I'd* rather be, not even Tahiti or the Riviera or Las Vegas—or Staten Island.

"Where can I find Mrs. Granby?" I said, hoping that she would be unfindable, but she wasn't.

"She lives over on Beal Hill, right up past Parsonfield's Funeral parlor. You can't miss Parsonfield's—there's three old rusty hearses in his front yard, with the wheels off. He's got a snowmobile hearse there, too."

"A *snowmobile* hearse?"

"Yeah, it's great in January and February and sometimes March, April, and May. He just Skidoos you up to the old graveyard and—"

"Why doesn't he just put skis on you and let you do a little cross-country on the way up to the old grave-

206

yard—you know, one last fling before—" I stopped in midflight as I saw Jock go for his frozen pickerel. "You think Mrs. Granby would help me?"

Jock relaxed, but he was still tense. "Yeah, she'd be glad to talk about the old days—and I mean the old *old* days. Old lady Granby is a hundred and eight."

"Oh, for Chrissakes," I said, "a hundred and eight! How's she gonna hear me when I ask a question?"

"She got a horn. She screws it into her good ear."

"Sure she does," I said, wishing that Granby Lakes had had another bar or even a McDonald's that bootlegged a little McBooze.

"Well, maybe she don't actually screw it in, but she shoves it down pretty far. I expect to see it come out the other side one of these days." Jock laughed at this because he was a closet sadist. He laughed at everything that hurt.

Mrs. Granby *was* old. There could be no doubt of that, but she greeted me with a handshake that stopped my John Cameron Swayze wristwatch. Sorry, John.

"Would you like a cup of tea?" she said, then shoved an old-fashioned ear trumpet so deep into her ear I was sure it would give her a cheap lobotomy. But apparently this was the only way she could hear.

"No thank you," I said.

"Good," she said. "I'll go put the kettle on." Maybe she should have shoved it a little deeper.

Mrs. Granby's "parlor" was like no other I had ever seen. She had a grand piano that looked as if it had been salvaged from the wreck of a British frigate off Cape Hatteras. Its three legs were buttressed with two-byfours painted red, white, and blue (in honor of a paint sale somewhere). The top of the grand piano was draped with a Spanish shawl that had seen better days— probably draped around Mrs. Granby's old shoulders at Jefferson's inaugural ball.

There was a field of framed photos covering most of the Spanish shawl and the top of the piano. They were, I reasoned, photographs of some of old Mrs. Granby's relatives. Or ancestors. Although, upon closer scrutiny, I recognized autographed pictures of Belle Starr, Lizzie Borden, John Dillinger, and the Manson family (who preceded *The Waltons* by a couple of years). There was even a self-consciously posed picture of Bonnie and Clyde (which may have been self-consciously posed because this time Clyde was smoking the cigar).

Other elements in Mrs. Granby's parlor impressed me that here was a woman of individual and far-out discrimination, not to mention an exquisite taste for the bizarre and unaffected Gongorism. The floor was covered wall to wall with welcome mats, probably purchased at a distress sale.

A Grecian urn stood precariously on a lavishly carved wooden pedestal. There was a faint inscription etched into its ceramicness: "This urn contains the ashes of my late and beloved husband, James—and also my late and beloved husband, Earl—and also my late and beloved husband, Fenimore. P.S. And Herkimer P. Babcock."

I expect no one to believe this, but there it was. I saw it. And, I hoped, someday to find out what Herkimer P. Babcock was doing in the same Grecian urn with Mrs. Granby's beloveds.

Mrs. Granby's parlor had further embellishments,

which would have taken half a lifetime to examine and catalogue.

Her bookcase contained only two books, *The Holy Bible* and *Charlie Chan and the Mystery of the Missing Mystery*. Mrs. Granby's taste in wallpaper was unique. A daisy-chain of queer cupids. Thousands of them. All clinging to each other with wildly satisfied, lascivious grins, and spelling out VIRTUE and ON WISCONSIN! A large grayish owl sat on a perch next to an old rocking chair. It could have been alive. I didn't try to find out. Between a corner whatnot case containing everything, it seemed, from stuffed turtles to petrified dinosaur dung (so marked) and fireplace complete with hanging pot, stood a television set. It must have been one of the first television sets ever made. It was an Atwater Kent and had fourteen tuning dials and a six-inch (measured diagonally) picture tube.

"Here we are." Mrs. Granby bounced in with a large tray holding a three-gallon teapot and two dainty cups and saucers and other tea-drinking accouterments.

"I was just admiring your television set," I said in a clumsy attempt at a pleasantry.

"Oh, yes," Mrs. Granby said. "Cream or lemon?"

"Is that a color TV set or a black and white?" Another idiotic remark.

"Neither," Mrs. Granby said. "One lump or two?"

"I don't understand," I said. "It's neither color nor black and white?"

"No."

"Then what is it?"

"I don't know," Mrs. Granby said. "I don't have any electricity here, so I don't know. If you want some entertainment, I'll play the piano for you. What would you like to hear?"

I would have liked very much to hear Mrs. Granby play the piano, after noticing how "gripped up" her hands were, possibly from arthritis. I really couldn't imagine how she could play at all, or (a wild thought) maybe she held a grapefruit in each hand and played like one of the Marx brothers used to play the piano, bashing the keys with the two grapefruits for a great comedic effect. I said, "I'd love to hear you play the piano, but—"

"Fine," she said, bouncing up, "I'll go get my grapefruit."

It took some doing, but I finally prevailed on old Mrs. Granby to hold off on the fruity concert until I asked her some questions.

"Mrs. Granby, I think I'd like to write a book about Granby Lakes. And from what I hear, you know more about this little town than anybody." (I felt she might be able to throw some light on the Sarah Selby Mansion problem.)

"I should. I'm a Granby, and I've lived here longer than anybody else, much longer. I'm ninety-six years old."

"Jock Lee said you were a hundred and eight," I said, ungallantly.

"Could be," Mrs. Granby said, becoming slightly vague for the first time. "But it doesn't matter. I guess I'll have to admit—I am getting old. I've outlasted four men—" She tapped the Grecian urn with her bamboo cane so that in a way explained Herkimer P. Babcock. "When I first came to Granby Lakes, I came as a bride—" Mrs. Granby's eyes brightened with a kind of soft sadness as she said this, and then looked toward the immensity of Granby Lake—stretching northward as far as you could see, disappearing into the darkening pines and spruce.

"I'll never forget James—James Granby. He was a direct descendant of Old Squire Granby. He was a giant of a man—six feet four—blond and blue-eyed, with dimples that showed deep when he smiled. He carried me across the threshold of our little log cabin with one hand, holding me on his hip like a sack of ripened grain. I remember him like it was yesterday. His smile, so full of love and warmth. His laugh, like thunder in the hills." Mrs. Granby wasn't talking to me now—she was talking to him.

"The cabin was beautiful. Huge bouldered fireplace. The furniture, made with James' own strong and knowing hands, gleaming with beeswax, and the lovely four-poster in the corner, covered with four-point Hudson's Bay Company blankets. The winters were long and cold, but we didn't mind. We had each other, and there was no other world but ours, and then there was the accident. I buried him myself. There was no choice. I was all alone in the middle of the vast wilderness. I planted a little pine tree at the head of James' grave. That little pine tree is a giant now—a tall, slender giant, like James was—"

I thought she was getting in a little deep, so I said, "Mrs. Granby, I didn't mean to bring up any sad—"

"And then there was Earl, my second—" Mrs. Granby continued without losing a beat. She went on through Earl and Fenimore, but she never mentioned Herkimer P. Babcock.

After Mrs. Granby had relived her life in instant replay, I asked her, "What was Granby Lakes like then?"

"You mean when I was a young bride?"

"Yes."

Old Mrs. Granby poured us some more tea, and she seemed to go into some sort of catatonic trance. Or else she had died. After what seemed like an era, I got up slowly and started to tiptoe toward the front door. I had made it a rule early in life—actually, it was one of my father's rules. "Never have tea with no dead old lady," he had warned me. I hadn't paid much heed to this sage admonition until now. And now it momentarily appeared to be just the situation he had been referring to so long ago. As I touched the door knob, old Mrs. Granby paddled back from across the Styx.

"Life in Granby Lakes, before Egil Grimshaw, was about as near as you could get to heaven without having to go through all that rigamarole first." This was the first indication that Egil Grimshaw was the first snake in this Furbish County Eden.

"You mean things changed after Egil Grimshaw came to Granby Lakes?" I said, hurrying back to the tea table, with my notebook open and my crayon poised.

"Egil Grimshaw bought the Granby Lakes bank for seven hundred and fifty dollars." I couldn't let the old lady get away with this, so I said, "Come on, Mrs. Granby, how could anyone buy a whole bank for seven hundred and fifty dollars?"

"It was easy. Egil Grimshaw married the Widow Stark. The Widow Stark owned the bank."

"Oh?"

"Yeah, then he started a development company, bought all the good acreage around Granby Lake."

212

"I don't know how long ago this was," I said, "but it must have taken a lot of money."

"Didn't take any," Mrs. Granby said, reaching for her snuffbox.

"It didn't?"

"No, the bank held the mortgage on all that good acreage. Egil Grimshaw just foreclosed on everybody." Mrs. Granby sneezed, blowing away her snuffbox.

"You mean nobody could pay up?"

"Not then. They were all farmers, and Egil Grimshaw had advised them to plant cotton on all that good acreage."

"Plant *cotton*—in *northern Maine!* And they *planted* it?"

"They sure did. Egil Grimshaw told them he read all about cotton in the *Farmer's Almanac,* and it would grow—even up here. And that's how Egil Grimshaw got the mortgage to their property. They all went broke because, just as the cotton plants were ready to bear, the thermometer dropped to ten above, and those thousands of acres of cotton turned blue overnight."

"It's a wonder they didn't come and get Egil Grimshaw and string him up to the nearest lamppost."

"They were thinking about it," Mrs. Granby said. "Someone brought it up at the town meeting, but it was voted down."

"Oh, come on now, Mrs. Granby!" I said. "They talked about a lynching at a town meeting? I can't believe it!"

"Well, go to a town meeting sometime. They're still talking about it. And all that happened fifty years ago."

"Why did they vote against it fifty years ago?"

"Because Egil Grimshaw showed it to 'em. It was right

there in the *Farmer's Almanac,* page 82—'Plant cotton in Granby Lakes on May 20th.'"

"That doesn't sound like the *Farmer's Almanac* to me," I said. "It's too specific."

"Doesn't sound right to me either," Mrs. Granby said, feeling around the floor for her snuffbox. "But I think it was because nobody else but Egil Grimshaw in Granby Lakes could read—he could have told them *anything!*"

That sounded logical because a lot of the Granby Lakes area folks can't read even today.

"Mrs. Granby, I'm a little puzzled—you say that Egil Grimshaw pulled off this land coup fifty years ago? Is this the same Egil Grimshaw that we have today? Doesn't seem quite—"

"Oh, good heavens, no. That was today's Egil Grimshaw's great-great-grandfather. The Egil Grimshaw we have today is the fourth one we've had."

"Jesus," I said, "it's like the twenty-year itch."

"Yes," Mrs. Granby said, "too bad they didn't have snowmobiles back in those days. Maybe the first or second or third Egil Grimshaw would have gone through the ice, and today we wouldn't have the fourth. And maybe life, like the song says, would be just a bowl of cherries."

"Yeah, instead of a carton of Kools," I said. This didn't make any sense, but it seemed to comfort old Mrs. Granby because she agreed with me wholeheartedly, and gave me some oatmeal cookies she had picked out at the IGA herself.

I talked to old Mrs. Granby for hours, and I learned a lot of the history of Granby Lakes, but very little about the old Sarah Selby Mansion.

Apparently nothing much happened until the first

Egil Grimshaw took over and succeeded where Old Squire Granby had failed. Egil Grimshaw sold the first development lot ever to be sold in Granby Lakes. He sold it to his mother, and later, when his mother failed to keep up her monthly payments, he foreclosed and took the property back. On Mother's Day.

Old Mrs. Granby filled me in about the present Egil Grimshaw. The now-residents of Granby Lakes looked upon him as the Great White Father, the village philanthropist. Even though they knew he was neither.

"Why does the village keep accepting these roads that go only to Egil Grimshaw's expensive development lots?" I asked old Mrs. Granby.

"It's the old New England spirit. They'll accept anything they think they're getting for nothing."

"But," I said, "these roads cost a fortune to pave and plow and fill in the potholes and smooth out the frost heaves—"

"Don't cost the town anything for that," Mrs. Granby said. "The summer residents and out-of-staters pay for all of it—taxes."

"That's ridiculous," I said, "the people who live here pay the same taxes as the summer residents and *out-of-staters*. They can't have two different rates for taxes!"

Old Mrs. Granby found her snuffbox and shoved a pinch up her little gray nose, then she started rocking slowly back and forth. Staring into space. I got up to go, and she did not seem to remember that I was there.

"I'll never forget Herkimer P. Babcock," she said, tapping the last name on her precious urn with her bamboo cane. "He was a giant of a man—six feet four, blond and blue-eyed, with dimples that showed deep when he smiled. He carried me across the threshold of our little

215

log cabin with one hand, holding me on his hip like a sack of ripened grain. I planted a little pine tree on his grave. . . ."

As I was leaving Mrs. Granby's place I noticed a lot of freshly planted little pine trees—maybe she *was* only ninety-six.

Five days and still Norman hadn't called.

30

SIX days and still Norman hadn't called, and as I ventured inside the post office to pick up my mail, the villagers seemed much more relaxed than they had been. They weren't any friendlier toward me, but the tension had gone. I visited the Town Office and found that Old Mrs. Granby was right about summer residents, out-of-staters, and other non-Maine natives paying more taxes than the locals. They (we) paid almost seven times as much as a local would have for the very same piece of real estate. I discovered this by going through the village tax list.

"Find out what you wanted to find out?" Miss LeGrand, the town clerk, smirked as I was leaving.

"Yes," I said, "we are being royally screwed!"

"Of course," she said, "but just look at those majestic mountains and that beautiful azure lake. God might have made a lovelier place than Granby Lakes, but He never did."

"Miss LeGrand," I said, "you have the soul of a poet. How much grass do you smoke a day?" Miss LeGrand didn't answer this. She just turned and walked back to her desk, her feet never once touching the floor.

Arriving back at Golgotha, North, I found a new health inspector prowling our kitchen, wearing virginly white gloves and touching everything that looked like it might be sooty.

"What the hell, Admiral," I said, "this ain't no submarine!"

"A kitchen in a Maine hotel must be cleaner than a submarine," the health inspector said without a modicum of facial expression. "This kitchen is filthy!"

"Who gives a good shit!?" I said, being at that point in my career as a hotel owner where I didn't care what they did to us. They had wanted to drive us crazy and they had succeeded.

"I'll have to close up your kitchen," the health inspector said, whipping out his little notebook and writing hurriedly, as I remembered the two magic words that seemed to work so well with the minions of Maine bureaucracy:

"Fuck off!" I said, about as sweetly as it's ever been said, then, with a little more hard-nose: "This isn't a hotel kitchen and you haven't got a goddamn thing to say about it! This is *our* kitchen and if we stand knee-deep in dead fish heads and never wash a goddamn plate, that's-the-way-it's-going-to-be-so-fuck-off!" After this, I must say, the health inspector fucked off, promptly.

We had been unable to get a temporary injunction barring Filthy Phil and his family from occupying our hotel. The reason we could not obtain this temporary injunction was lost somewhere in legal bibble-babble, which our new lawyer was careful not to explain. It was his little secret.

The lawyer's failure to get a temporary injunction did nothing to instill confidence in our being able to get a *permanent* one, although he assured us that there would be no problem, and our very unwelcome guests would

218

be out for good. Our court appearance had been set for sometime the following month, but this didn't help us much at the moment. Filthy Phil and his onerous brood were still bedded down in the hotel, along with Reiko, me, and our kids. And all of us, by this time, were wearing flea collars. The kind that also killed rats, bats, and mice.

There were other distractions, besides Filthy Phil's road company infestation, which scraped our nerves raw.

The villagers of Granby Lakes had closed ranks and were now as one—against the Honeymoon Mountain Inn. The Chamber of Commerce, ever helpful, had posted a friendly warning to any tourist who might drop into their tiny office for a bit of information about where to spend the night in Granby Lakes. Mrs. Quinzel, the head of the Chamber, volunteered that Honeymoon Mountain Inn was to be highly recommended—if the tourist had been inoculated against the Black Plague. And yaws.

Most tourists didn't seem to be too concerned about the Black Plague, according to my little informer, Betsy Couzy, but to them "yaws" sounded ominous, and they avoided the Honeymoon Mountain Inn in droves. And I really *couldn't* blame them because by this time there was even a dead cow in the front yard. How it got there I don't know, but apparently, with Filthy Phil, this was about all he had to offer as a status symbol.

Reiko, Bobby, Timothy, and I were the new Leningrad—besieged on three sides by the enemy. The fourth side contained the dead cow. "Things" were happening to us every day and in every way. We *must* go! That's all there was to it. Our insane stubbornness must be cured right now! Granby Lakes had always triumphed before and it would again!

Mr. Titterford, the jolly fat slob who owned the Titterford Hill Dairy, visited us several times when we were not home and claimed some more of his dairy equipment, such as a Waring mixer, a sterilizer, and three bottles of J&B Scotch. Filthy Phil was only too glad to let Mr. Titterford have what he wanted because Filthy Phil owed Mr. Titterford seventy-six dollars for the cow who died.

The Granby Lakes Power Company rates went up 34 percent (for us alone) because of the increased cost of fossil fuel. The Granby Lakes Power Company kept it a deep dark secret that they used only water from a dammed-up river to generate their power. They'd never heard about fossil fuel until they read about it in *Cosmopolitan* (Helen Gurley Brown had run an article about coal being good for the skin), but they latched onto any excuse to get their rate up where it would be worthwhile. Also, they wanted another seven-hundred-and-fifty-dollar deposit from a *new* owner, and we were upsetting their schedule. We counterattacked by turning off the furnace motors and using our monstrous fireplace, burning only Granby Lakes Power Company bills.

"Gee," Reiko said, hanging up the telephone receiver, "guess what? I have a reservation for twenty-four people tonight. They want lobster, caviar, champagne, and everything."

"My God!" I said. I was astonished. "Who's coming —Lee Radziwill?"

"Who?"

"It's a name I made up," I said.

"It's a dinner party for the *governor!* I've got to really hustle," Reiko said. "Gotta get a couple of girls to serve. Champagne we have. Caviar and lobster—where can we get caviar?" Which was really a very stupid question to ask way up in our region.

"How about Boston?" I suggested.

"Would you mind driving all that way?" she asked.

"Five hours there and five hours back? Not at all." Then I shot myself.

We didn't get the caviar, but everything else was ready. This fancy dinner party was set for eight o'clock. By twelve thirty we realized that nobody was going to appear. I checked the newspaper. The governor was in Puerto Rico warming up for a Maine winter.

There really wasn't too much these hecklers overlooked, and after a while we thought it was funny, or else we were on the verge of terminal hysteria. I didn't know what was real and what was imagined. At that stage it was hard to tell. In my half-world between real and unreal I got named in a paternity suit by a thirty-six-year-old humpbacked midget. She said I took advantage of her on New Year's Eve. Not that it matters what night, but I had to go to court and swear that she wasn't pregnant at all. She had just pushed her hump around to the front so she could blackmail me. The judge asked her if she had ever taken the rabbit test and she said no—she had to draw the line somewhere.

I don't want to strain your credulity or belabor this whole thing, but they tried a new version of something they had done before. They had Charlie Ferguson, the modern town crier, who had the loudspeaker on his old beat-up Pontiac rolling back and forth along Main Street yelling at the top of his one lung that Mick Jagger and the Rolling Stones, Johnny Cash, and Linda Lovelace were going to be at the Honeymoon Mountain Inn that night. In person!

I didn't think that that old cornball trick would work again, but it did. It seemed that people were desperate to *believe,* and thousands of them showed up to see these great stars.

We tried in vain to explain that this was all news to us, but they wouldn't go away. They were sure that Filthy Phil was Mick Jagger and insisted that Mick tie the confederate flag onto his well-publicized *thing* and wave it in six-eight time while they all sang "On Top of Old Smoky." Filthy Phil was all for it and said he'd be glad to do it, with not only one, but *two* flags *and* a small pennant. *And* a string of Christmas light bulbs.

We locked him in a closet.

And the crowd thought that Filthy Phil's daughter, Jezebel, who was undressing, as usual, before an open window with the shades up, was Linda Lovelace. I tried to take advantage of this and charge them a small fee to watch her, but they wouldn't pay until I went upstairs and asked Jezebel if she'd mind eating a banana in the nude. She didn't mind at all, and, after that, I passed the hat and collected almost seven dollars.

We got obscene phone calls from President Ford and Princess Grace, or so they said. And Golda Meir.

Our swimming pool was filled one night with some Amazonian piranha that ate three guests (thank God we had forgotten to register them). Getting rid of their car was another story, and this may strain your credulity again, but it took us five weeks. Our garbage compacter could only digest a very small part of a Toyota bus every day. Sometimes it would throw up and we'd have to start all over again.

The most discouraging part of this whole period was when we had more guests than we had expected, and by keeping the Filthy Phil family locked in the basement, we managed to hang on to them—until this Maine guide came along and solicited us for business. He took all of our guests on a fishing-hunting-camping trip and we never saw any of them again.

That did it! Just as the sun was setting, Norman called:

Jack? . . . Norman. . . . They're back!"

"Oh no!"

"Yes, and there are a lot more of them now—must be a couple of thousand, at least!"

"A couple of thousand!"

"Yes, and these are much bigger than the other ones, much bigger. They must be at least eighteen or twenty feet tall, counting their feelers."

"Feelers?" I was amazed. "You mean they're some kind of—"

"Hold it!" Norman stopped me. "They're all starting to move in one giant mass. They're crawling across the big clearing near the swamp. Oh, no!"

"What happened?"

"One of them just caught a moose, and ate it in one big bite!"

"A full-grown moose?"

"Yeah, horns and all! Christ! These are the biggest ants I've ever seen!"

"Ants!?" I said.

"Ants!!!" It was a woman's voice. Alma, the operator.

"What are they doing now?" I said.

"They're crawling downhill."

"Looking for more moose?"

"No, they're moving very fast now, heading right for the village!"

"The *village!*" Alma shrieked, and the phone went dead.

I walked out on the observation deck of the inn, looking toward the village. In no less than seven minutes, a stream of cars, bright headlights on, were heading south, driving like the start of the Indianapolis Five Hundred. Filthy Phil got a call, and he and his family streaked out the driveway as if the very hounds of hell were after them. I didn't think his 1934 pickup had that kind of speed.

I waited exactly one hour and everything was very quiet, then I drove down to the village with my six hundred pounds of fresh cow manure, and went joyfully to work, depositing a large shovelful in the middle of the living room of each of the ninety-seven houses in the village. At dawn I drove back to the Honeymoon Mountain Inn with a heart full of the thought of happy accomplishment, a dream fulfilled.

We had almost a whole week of peace and lovely quiet, then cautiously the good folk of Granby Lakes started to trickle back to their hastily abandoned homes.

"Did anyone *see* these giant ants?" I asked Betsy Couzy, when she came to me with the story.

"No," she said, "but they all know that they had *been* there!"

224

CHAPTER

31

TROUBLE returned with the villagers, and Emil LaBoute, our new and, I felt, trustworthy, lawyer counseled us every day. Or maybe the word isn't "counseled"—better, he "consoled" us and also "cooled" us. He had to cool me because I was all for spreading a little gasoline around Main Street and dropping a lighted native into it. In northern New England villages burned down every other day, so I felt that nobody would notice that Granby Lakes was gone. (Along with us.)

We now had four problems, which could only be settled in court before a judge (preferably Solomon). The land that Mr. Tolland sold us, through Egil Grimshaw's real estate brokerage, was described in the deed as being twenty acres, more or less. This "more or less" clause seemed to have cut us down to 4.51 acres, more or less. Thomas E. Yates, the golf course owner, claimed that he owned the road (our driveway) and that it was part of his golf course. And, according to his lawyer, he had the papers to prove it. Problem number three was Miss Harriet Quimpy, who, by sheer mindless persistence, had collected a lot of schoolchildren's pennies toward the purchase of the Honeymoon Mountain Inn, to be given to the state and renamed the Sarah Selby Historic Shrine. Or the Sarah Selby Historic Shrine Whorehouse, whichever was considered appropriate. Rumor had it that the government was about to condemn the place so we'd be forced to sell. At what price we did not know, but, in previous dealings with authority, I have never been paid what I expected from any condemnation. (I had once owned a California ranch that had been condemned for use as a gunnery range, and although the man with the condemnation documents said I would get five hundred dollars per acre, I received only two hundred per—and I had paid seven hundred and fifty.) If these California prices seem low to you, don't forget: When I owned that California ranch, California still belonged to Mary Pickford.

Filthy Phil Selby and his malodorous mob had returned and were our main concern. Because he was a Selby, no matter how many times removed from the original Sarah, we were haunted by the spector of some thin line of credibility in his claim. Because, by this time, we knew that Joseph F. Fulman did not do a title search when we took over. Why Filthy Phil had never made the slightest move toward claiming his inheritance, of course, was a matter of conjecture. A conjecture which certainly was no great mystery. Filthy Phil (if he had any legitimate claim) simply had not known about it until he was sneakily informed by someone.

"But who?" Reiko asked.

"I don't know yet," I said, "but I think we can eliminate Egil Grimshaw on this one."

"You mean, this dirty trick is on someone else?" Bobby said. This was astounding in itself.

"Sure, if Grimshaw brought it up, he would be on the hook for representing the place as free and clear. He's the one who did the title search on it when he—or, more correctly, his bank—sold it to Thomas E. Yates. Then

226

Yates sold it to Tolland, and Tolland sold it to us. None of them actually had any right to sell it, and it all goes back to Grimshaw, so he'd never open his face about it. Neither would Yates or Tolland."

"How about Old Miss Harriet Quimpy?"

"Yeah," I said, "Old Miss Harriet. She wants this place so badly, even as an historic Pussy Shrine. She probably got to Filthy Phil and convinced him that the Honeymoon Mountain Inn was rightfully his."

"Maybe it is."

"Yeah, and Old Miss Harriet is a sharpy. She knows that she can't raise enough pennies from school kids to buy this place from us. But Filthy Phil would be a pushover. He'd probably let it go for a couple of hundred bucks and a bottle of muscatel."

This gave the Granby Lakes villagers a lot to think about. If Old Miss Harriet carried the day, the Honeymoon Mountain Inn would no longer be a financial asset, unless the Granby Lakers could do to the United States government what they had been doing since 1923 to the forty-nine other owners. The consensus, I learned from Betsy Couzy, my very own CIA, was that they would rather do battle with us than Uncle Sam. Uncle Sam might be too tough for Granby Lakes, Betsy Couzy told me. I didn't think so.

The uncertainty of the moment was unbearable, and we looked to our day in court. Win or lose. Thumbs up or down. Anything would have been better than the tightrope we were walking. The resentment against us was smoldering into a conflagration, for having put Granby Lakes in such a disadvantageous position. From our mountaintop, far above it, we could see a bright halo of hate, rising up from the village. Or so it seemed in our rapidly disintegrating reason. Once in a while, waiting for our court appearance at the Furbish County courthouse, in Strunkville, we had periods of some lucidity.

We knew we would have to put up a strong defense against the claim of a Selby who was claiming his ancestral home. But any kind of defense in a lawsuit takes money. Even a token defense. And, with the little money we had left, it looked like our defense was going to be very token.

"Don't throw good money after bad!" our accountant, Henry Rosemont, said (Henry was an avid reader of *Words to Live By*), but Henry's advice came a little late. We had already thrown most of our bad money and all of our good money. We were deep in a hole of our own digging. Always a Monday morning quarterback, I knew we shouldn't have burned all the empty United Van Lines wardrobe, dish, and book boxes. In fact, we should never have unpacked. Or packed.

I thought of borrowing from some of my wealthy friends, but they had already borrowed from their wealthy friends. I tried to think what kind of work I was suited for, as a sideline.

"Maybe you could become a Bunny. They make a lot of money," suggested Earl Harkins, the village drunk, one night in our bar.

"You're a big help," I said. "Thanks, Earl." Earl's feelings were hurt, and he was going to leave, but because he was our only bar patron that night, I wanted to keep him there. He never paid for his drinks because, he explained, driving a school bus didn't put him in the same financial stratosphere as an airline pilot.

"How could I become a Bunny? Who the hell would believe me?"

"Well," Earl reasoned, "you gotta pick your spots—like maybe the old men's home over to Farmington. They need a Bunny."

"My God!" I said.

"You like the idea, huh?" Earl said, pouring most of his bourbon and Coke up his nose, which didn't seem to hamper his wassailing any. "You could wear a couple of half-filled hot water bottles, black pantyhose, and glue an English muffin to your ass. Them old bastards over to Farmington would never know the difference—unless one of them got hungry."

I thanked Earl for his sagacity, poured another bourbon and Coke up his nose and went to bed.

The next morning I remembered some MGM stock we could sell, but nobody was investing in MGM since Jim Aubrey sold Judy Garland's little red slippers. People had just lost faith in America after that. Watergate meant nothing alongside this heartless betrayal of trust.

"No, Jack," Egil Grimshaw in his role as the local bank president said, after tolerating my request for a lower interest rate and longer-term mortgage. "The bank's policy is never to change the interest rate once it is established, and term of the mortgage can neither be lengthened or shortened. We decided that at a board meeting." He then stroked his baby-blue suspenders and flicked an inquisitive horsefly off his green-shirted belly, which resembled an untidy front lawn.

"What board meeting?"

"*The* board meeting!" Egil said, doing a quick change-over from the avuncular to the Gulag Archipelago.

"Oh," I said, and hung right in there, "who's on the board?"

Egil had recovered and was back-stroking his baby-blue suspenders silly. "Well, there's Poseidon and—" As soon as he named his nonexistent partner, I knew the rest of the board names would be even more imaginative.

"Thanks, anyway, Mr. Grimshaw," I said, "and—" As I was leaving this hallowed hall of horseshit, I stopped and turned, in the manner of Columbo: "Just one more thing—not important, of course—"

This brought the baby-blue-suspender stroking to an abrupt halt, and Egil Grimshaw half rose from behind the fortress of his desk, alert as a mother weasel protecting its young. "What's that?"

"About the deed—and the map of our property—"

"What about it?"

"Seems like two—*different*—pieces of property." I knew I had struck a nerve because Egil Grimshaw started strapping on a belt to shore up his suspenders. He didn't quite make it with the belt. It was too short.

"Maybe you oughta try a cinch."

"What was that?"

"You know, a cinch around your belly, like Secretariat wears—makes him look *taller*—"

Egil ignored this helpful hint on men's wear and said, "So that's how you think you're gonna wriggle outa the deal, huh? The old 'two different pieces of property bit,' huh?" I had no idea of what the "old two pieces of property bit" meant because I hadn't lived in this region that long.

"Mr. Grimshaw," I said, "I don't want to wriggle out of the deal. Wriggling out of the deal is the furthest thing from my mind. It's the sweetest deal in the world, and you've helped so much with all your little kindnesses to make it so. I was merely pointing out these

230

minor differences in the map and deed. They're very minor, very minor. The property lines can't be off more than a couple of hundred feet or so. And what difference does it make whether we own four-and-a-half acres or twenty acres—like it is on the map—so long as our little, itty-bitty, teeny-tiny four-and-a-half acres are really *ours*—and *ours alone.*"

"Yeah," Egil Grimshaw agreed, "a map don't mean a thing. It's what it says in the deed. Yeah, that's it. It's what it says in the deed that counts, just what it says in the deed." Egil Grimshaw seemed to have fallen in love with this "what it says in the deed" phrase. He kept repeating it over and over, first to me and, after I started out the door, to himself. I had no way of knowing, but I felt that he would be repeating it to himself all day long, maybe making up a little melody to go with it, so he could sing it softly to his little record book of Honeymoon Mountain Inn foreclosures.

"Well?" Reiko wanted to know as soon as I walked into the living room and flung myself down onto a three-hundred-dollar section of our five thousand dollars' worth of terraced wall-to-wall carpeting.

"Waddya mean, *well?*" I said, in a tone that was a sure-fire prelude to a screaming contest. Every discussion about the Honeymoon Mountain Inn had become a screaming contest, but this time it was different. Reiko was icily calm. "He said no, huh?"

"That's it," I said. "But I think I ruffled him a bit when I mentioned the discrepancy between the deed and the property map."

"What's 'discrepancy'?" Reiko asked.

"It means that the deed and the map are different. The deed—if that goddamn tricky lawyer Fulman had

taken the time to read it and explain it to us—means
that we have only four-and-a-half acres of ground, and
the map from which the property was sold to us—long
before we'd seen any deed—gives us twenty acres. Then
Grimshaw tells me that only what it says in the deed is
significant."

"What's 'significant'?"

"It means, the deed is the only thing that counts. It's
the only thing that has any definity, any graphicness."

"Oh," Reiko said, "I see." When Reiko says, "I see," I
knew from thousands of experiences that she didn't remotely understand.

"What's 'definity' and 'graphicness'?"

"Jesus Christ!" I said, impatient with Reiko's understandable puzzlement.

"It's funny," she said, "when Americans get mad, they
say, 'Jesus Christ!'"

"What's funny about it?"

"In Japan, when we get mad, we never say 'Buddha!'"

I thought about this.

I had been in court only once before in my hectic lifetime, even though I had pulled a few unlawful acts. Triv-
ial, but against the law. During the Great Experiment
in futility, I had delivered, prohibited by the Volstead
Act, cases of rotgut to eager consumers. At the time, of
course, no one considered this to be an illegal or uneth-
ical procedure. I didn't, and if I did—I needed the
money, which was unworthy of serious consideration,
except that I could buy myself a hot dog and an occasional Orange Julius, to keep body and soul together.

232

Why they should be kept *together* is something I was never able to learn at Billy Graham's sacrosanct knee. This was before he got to be a television star and crusading all over hell, trying to convince people that hell wasn't endorsed by *Good Housekeeping.* Yet.

My only court appearance was during the time I was playing the nun to Lenny Bruce's priest in Miami Beach. We got pinched for soliciting funds for a glassed-in leper colony, which, we told people, was planned for one corner of the lobby in the Hotel Fontainebleau, to show the guests what it was like at the other Miami Beach hotels. Lenny and I had collected almost nine hundred dollars from passing gentiles, when we were deterred by the law (such as it is in Miami Beach) and had to give the nine hundred dollars back, the judge said. When Lenny told the judge we had picked up this money from people passing by in the street and we couldn't possibly know who they were or where they were, the judge, who was very understanding, said that, nevertheless, we were to go out and find those people and give them their money back. If we didn't, we would be in contempt of court, so we had no choice. It took Lenny and me almost seven years to find nine hundred gentiles in Miami Beach. And we had to pay them fifty cents each to admit it.

Now I was in court for the second time in my life. The Furbish County Court as presided over by Judge Avon Bean. Just in passing, in order to be a county court judge in Northern Maine your name had to be either Bean, Quimpy, Hinkley, or Dunham. This was not a guarantee, but it gave you a helluva headstart.

Everybody, except a large flea-scratching dog, stood

up when Judge Avon Bean entered the stiflingly hot small courtroom and whacked his gavel on the splintery desk to make sure the gavel was working.

"What have we got here?" the judge wanted to know. A tall cadaverous man stood up and enunciated in stentorian tones, "Hear Ye! Hear Ye! Hear Ye! the first Circuit Court of Furbish County is now in session, Judge Avon Bean presiding, all rise."

"Jesus, Henry," the judge snorted, "where the hell have you been—we shoulda done that first! *Before* I came in!"

"You wanna do it over?" the cadaver said. The judge's answer came in the form of a long nose-blow. It seemed either he had a bad cold or he was warming up to play "The Boogie-Woogie Bugle Boy from Company B." Or maybe both.

"What's the matter with the judge's nose?" Reiko whispered.

"He's got sinus trouble," Goldie Renk, our attorney, who was substituting for Emil LaBoute, who was busy on another rape case, whispered back, "and he's got sinuses like the Carlsbad Caverns."

Joseph F. Fulman had openly (this time) joined the opposition. Not that he had much choice: We had named him in our complaint about the shitty deal we had got from him, Egil Grimshaw, and Mr. Tolland, the former owner. Or as the complaint read:

> The defendants, together and separately, have willfully conspired, colluded, contrived, connived, and machinated to give the Honeymoon Mountain Inn a shitty deal.

That is as near the legal language as I can remember. "What seems to be the trouble here?" Judge Avon Bean said, in a tone which brought back scenes from Paul Newman's movie about the *hanging* judge, *Roy* Bean. Avon sounded as if he might be a relative. He never glanced over at our corner, but he smiled benignly at the opposition as they lolled about the courtroom looking like they owned it. And they might just as well have owned it, the way things started to go—for us—almost immediately. One of the first problems dealt with the area size of the land we had bought, and the small chunk we apparently wound up with. The judge—still not looking at Reiko or me or Bobby and Timothy, whom we had brought along to show them what they would be up against, as their lives progressed—said, "What would you people do with all that land anyway?"

Goldie Renk, who was supposed to be representing us, said nothing, so I answered, "All what land, Your Honor?"

"All *what* land?" the judge muttered. "Jesus Christ, what are we here for? The land which is in dispute! The four-and-one-half acres your hotel is setting on!"

"Er—Your Honor," I said, not quite believing that this old fart didn't know anything about the case, "we are not here in the matter of the four-and-a-half acres which our hotel is 'setting' on. We are here because we bought twenty acres, and now—according to those people over there—own only four-and-a-half. That's a difference of fifteen-and-a-half acres—"

"I can subtract," the judge said impatiently, "so answer the question. What would you do with all that

235

land? You're from out of state, aren't you?"

"What's that got to do with it?" *I* was getting snippy now.

"Watch it there, feller!" the judge said. "You can be held for contempt of court! Very easily."

"Contempt of court, my ass," I said, quite softly, I'll admit.

"What was that?" the judge said, turning up his hearing aid.

"Judge," I said, "we paid for twenty acres of land and we'd like to have it."

"What does the deed say?" the judge asked.

"It sure doesn't say twenty acres."

"We gotta go by the deed."

"But, Judge," I said, "when you buy a piece of property, you don't even see a deed. They keep it a big secret. All you see is a map, and you see boundary markers, put out by the seller or the real estate people. You don't see any deed until closing time—when you hand over your hard-earned cash!"

"Whaddya do, feller?" was the judge's next question.

"I'm a writer," I said. "You know, books, television, anything that comes along."

"Oh," the judge said, still not looking in my direction. But I thought his tone was more gentle. "A writer, huh?" Then mostly to himself: "The things that have happened in this courtroom—*I* could write a book."

"Why don't you, Your Honor," I said, sensing a small chink in his crinkled armor. "I think you could write a very good book."

"Yeahhh . . ." The judge liked this. He liked this very much. "Now, let's get back to the case. What did you say you were going to do with all this land?"

236

"You mean the four-and-a-half acres or the twenty acres?"

"Who the hell cares? Land is land. It should be used."

"It is being used, by our hotel. We gotta have a little land around it."

The judge blew his nose again. This time the American flag riffled a little and a picture of Martha Washington fell off the wall.

"In other words," the judge finally continued, "you are letting this land lay fallow. No crops. No corn. No beans. No Brussels sprouts—"

"We have dandelions," Timothy said.

The judge whipped around in our direction. "Who said that? Have him removed from the courtroom at once. This is a court of law, and there shall be dignity at all times. Dignity! Is that clearly understood???!!!" Then he blew his nose again and fucked up any dignity left in the world.

The trial was as everyone on our side (a small group) clichéd it—a mockery of justice. Reiko and I and the Honeymoon Mountain Inn didn't have a prayer, and Goldie Renk, who spouted so much law *before* he got to the courtroom, like a fountain piped directly into Blackstone, said nary a word.

When it was over, the judge, Joseph F. Fulman, Mr. Tolland, and Egil Grimshaw all went out the back door to the Bide-a-Wee Cocktail Lounge together, laughing and slapping each other on the back. Reiko and I and Timothy and Bobby sat with Goldie Renk in our car, silently. Very silently. The whole thing was too much, so after a while, I had to ask Goldie, "Why the hell didn't you open your mouth?"

"The judge is my wife's father," Goldie said. "He

doesn't believe I'm a lawyer. He just laughs and takes another drink every time I tell him."

Sic transit gloria mundi, which means, if you have to go to court in Maine and you don't happen to be a native son, forget it. Instead, just throw yourself in front of a fat girls' roller derby team—during a sprint.

CHAPTER

32

"LET'S go back to Connecticut or Canada—or any-where—and forget this whole thing," Reiko said. She was low. Very low. And so was I, but my zodiac sign told me I was stubborn and tenacious and determined. It didn't say anything about my being naïve, gullible, de-ludeable, and stupid. But I guess the zodiac never tells anybody anything unpleasant or they'd be out of busi-ness in no time.

"I'd love to get the hell out of here," I said, "but we can't. We've got to stay and fight. We've got to get back some of the money we threw away on this place. And we can't get it by running off."

"I don't think we're going to get it in court either. That Judge Bean hates us. Maybe he hates me because I'm Japanese. Maybe he was in the war. Maybe he hates Gooks."

"*Gooks!*" I said. "Where'd you get *that* word?"

"From Bobby—he's writing a story for school, he said, about me. It's called, 'My Mother, the Gook.'"

I learned later that Mrs. Abernathy, Bobby's seventh-grade teacher, used this word to describe all Orientals, which was certainly a thoughtful step in the direction of a better understanding among the peoples of the world. Amen.

* * *

The Furbish County Court was jammed with Granby Lakers the day of our second appearance. This was to determine if Filthy Phil Selby had any claim on the real estate we had bought from Mark Tolland. The first episode of how many acres we owned (according to the deed) had been settled at four and one half, which really didn't give the deer and the antelope much room to play. Not that we had any deer or antelope. All we had (for wildlife) was a three-legged fox who used to drink out of our swimming pool at dusk. Presumably he had only three legs because he had been caught in one of the new "humane" animal traps. These new traps don't kill; they just take off one leg. And sitting there in the crowded courtroom, awaiting the arrival of Judge Avon Bean, we were about to lose more than a leg. I have never been an optimist, but also I have never been so aware of the futility of it all. This "all" being the system of Furbish County justice, which had no resemblance to justice as practiced in the rest of New England.

Furbish County had two separate methods of dealing with legal problems, based on where you were born. I knew that my entry into the world at Smith's Infirmary in Port Richmond, Staten Island, wouldn't influence anybody in Furbish County to give me any loud "Hip-Hip Hurrays" or even a faint "Banzai!"

The tall cadaver we had seen in our first court 'appearance had sneaked in surreptitiously, as if trying to catch the crowd off-guard. He announced in a voice even more stentorian than the first time: "The First Circuit Court of Furbish County is now in session, Judge Avon Bean presiding, all rise!" We all rose, but nothing happened. We stood for at least twelve minutes, waiting in vain for Judge Avon Bean. No Judge Avon Bean.

240

Some of the more daring sat down. And soon all of us were sitting down. It was hot, it was sticky, and it was nothing like *Perry Mason,* and we knew that no Perry Mason assistant would rush in at the last minute with the information that new evidence had been found and the defendants (us) would be home free. I wished we had never left Canada or Connecticut or anywhere. We might be safe now, and maybe even cool.

Judge Avon Bean suddenly popped up—like he was on jack-in-the-box springs—from behind the bench. He caught everybody by surprise, even the cadaver who was supposed to announce him, which, I think, from the sly look on his face, was the judge's intention.

"Jesus Christ, Avon, where you been?" the cadaver said. The judge whacked his gavel a few times and announced, "Hear Ye! Hear Ye! Hear Ye! The First Circuit Court of Furbish County is now in session. Judge Avon Bean presiding, all rise!" Everyone, except the scratching dog, who seemed to be in residence in the courtroom, scrambled up. One old man began to sing "Glory, Glory, Hallelujah" very loudly and very off-key. The judge whacked his gavel again, and the old man stopped as suddenly as he had begun. "Hell!" the old man mumbled.

"Shut up, Mitch, you son of a bitch!" the judge said, then he chuckled. He had tickled himself. "I like that," he said. "'Shut up, Mitch, you son of a bitch'—Parley-vous." He was now singing to the tune of "Hinky-Dinky Parlay-voo," "Shut up, Mitch, you son of a bitch—parley-vous—" Suddenly he stopped and asked, "Anybody here remember World War One?" No one, apparently, did.

"What's the first case on the docket, deputy?" The

241

judge was all-business now. The first case on the docket was Filthy Phil Selby as the plaintiff and Reiko and I as the defendants. Miss Harriet Quimpy was the first witness. And since she spoke for almost five hours without letup, she was the only witness. And Reiko and I lost the case. The Honeymoon Mountain Inn was the sole property of Filthy Phil Selby. There could be no doubt, Judge Bean had said, and we were inclined to go along. Miss Quimpy had produced document after document, ancient deed after ancient deed, all relieving us of our hotel-motel and surrounding buildings.

As soon as we were outside the courtroom, surrounded by the sea of smirking faces attached to the Granby Lakers, I said, "I'm going to kill Joseph F. Fulman!"

"Why?" Goldie Renk, who still seemed to be our lawyer and no help at all, said. "He didn't do anything."

"That's why," I said. "He didn't search the deed and get us a free and clear title."

"But he guaranteed us a free and clear title," Reiko said.

"Yeah," Goldie Renk said, "so you won't have to kill him, just sue him."

"Just sue him?" I said, sardonically, I hoped.

"Yeah."

"In Furbish County?!"

"Why not?" I didn't bother to answer this or even think about it. I might have killed Goldie Renk, just to set an example to some of the other Furbish County lawyers. It might make them think twice before they screwed you. It really wouldn't stop them from screwing you, but thinking twice would delay it a bit.

"Where on earth did Miss Quimpy get all those old papers and deeds and all that legal stuff?" Reiko wanted to know. So did I. So did the world.

"Christ!" I said. "All the deeds and stuff like that is supposed to be recorded at the County Courthouse. Why wasn't it?" We can't blame Joseph F. Fulman if that stuff wasn't there, even if he did look for it, which, of course, he didn't.

"I think," Goldie Renk said, "that those were the original deeds. The copies, which were undoubtedly recorded, must have been at the *old* County Courthouse."

"What do you mean—the 'old' County Courthouse?"

"The one that burned down in 1813."

"Oh?"

"And in 1846—1872—1898—1903—1926—and 1931."

When Reiko, Bobby, Timothy, and I drove into the driveway of the Honeymoon Mountain Inn, all the lights were on and there were sounds of much revelry coming from the living room and bar.

The front door was locked and my key would not open it. This should have told us something, but it didn't. I knocked on the door with my key ring. Nothing happened. I knocked again, this time harder. No one heard us. I kicked the door with my heavy woods boots. After the eighth or ninth kick, the door opened. It was Filthy Phil Selby himself. "Sorry, folks," he said, "but this is a private party." Then he slammed the door shut. I kicked the door for a good twenty minutes after this, but it was never opened again.

We spent the night at the Sugarback Motor Inn, a motel some thirty-five miles away.

243

CHAPTER

33

I have never taken foxy pills, but the next morning while the sun was just coming up—all pink and silver— over Sugarback Mountain, I was at the hotel, taking advantage of Filthy Phil's soul-shredding hangover, buying the place back from him for thirty-five hundred dollars. He signed the receipt, which I had made out with his name and the amount and what it was for, and by breakfast time, with more money than he knew existed, Filthy Phil, his sludgy wife, Mona, and his five verminous offspring had gone back to their tarpaper shack at the gateway to Granby Lakes, and we were once again the proud (?) owners of the Honeymoon Mountain Inn, and Miss Harriet Quimpy was in a state of shock, lying in the couch in our living room. She never expected to see *us*. She planned, as we had, to catch Filthy Phil on the verge of delirium tremens and offer him even more than we had, and all in pennies. (She had a dump-truck load of them parked right outside.) But our expeditious return made her flip entirely, and now she was under sedation—six aspirins and a menopause martini (a martini with a mothball instead of an olive).

Our next visitor on that busy early morning was Egil Grimshaw. He wanted to make a deal.

"What kind of a deal?"

"Well," Egil said, rubbing his baby-blue suspenders for luck, "a deal that'll get you off the hook and make you a lot of money."

"We've heard that before," Reiko said.

"Wanna see our dead cow?" Timothy said. "We just bought it." Egil Grimshaw ignored Timothy and said, "I'll give you then ten thousand more than you paid for the place."

"Fuckermother!" Timothy said.

"Fifteen thousand," Egil said quickly.

"You know something, don't you?" I asked.

"Of course, I do," Egil said, smiling and rubbing.

The something that Egil Grimshaw knew was a very strong rumor that Harriet Quimpy had done her work well, and even though Senators Muskie, Jackson, Proxmire, Goldwater, and Kennedy had laughed the whole thing off as a big put-on, one newly elected representative from somewhere, who had the voice of a bull and the guts of Bella Abzug, had arranged somehow for the U.S. government to appropriate two hundred thousand dollars to buy the Old Sarah Selby Mansion and designate it as a National Historic Shrine—the First Whorehouse in America. No wonder Egil Grimshaw was willing to give us fifteen thousand more than we paid.

I wish I could say that we knew all about the government's generous throwing around of our IRS contributions, but we did not and we agreed to Egil Grimshaw's offer and had accepted his check for $25 as "earnest money." Earnest money, for you initiated, means money paid by the buyer to the seller to prove that he is sincere, and Egil Grimshaw proved that he was willing to part with at least $25 worth of sincerity, which is about as much sincerity as you'll get in Granby Lakes. Compassion is a little more: $27.50.

"What about the road—our driveway?" Reiko asked Grimshaw. "How can we sell this place without a way to get to it?"

"Yeah," I said, "Mr. Yates, the golf course owner, says he owns our road because it goes to his golf course. He's using it now for not only his golf customers, but for trucks, Greyhound buses, sightseeing tours, motorcycle gangs, Winnebago campers, and so on forever, and now the crooked son of a bitch is suing us to prevent us from using it! That prince of a fellow is a prince of a prick!"

"I agree," Egil Grimshaw said, "but I'll take care of that, so don't worry. I know just how to handle him." And he did. He knew more than he'd ever let on. We found out later that *he* had sold both *us* and *Mr. Yates* the road in question, which wouldn't have been so bad if it had been his to sell, but details, like *who* owned *what*, had never bothered Egil Grimshaw in all of his wheelings and dealings in Granby Lakes. If you wanted a piece of property, he'd sell it to you because he knew it might be years before the real owner would discover that it had been sold. By that time Grimshaw might be old enough to plead senility, or if it was discovered immediately, Grimshaw would be having a heart attack in Florida—or whatever ailment came first to his mind. Florida was his San Clemente when things went wrong.

Three days after Egil Grimshaw's offer giving us fifteen thousand dollars above what we had paid for the Honeymoon Mountain Inn, the deal was off and Egil

Grimshaw wanted his $25 earnest money back. And he was very sincere about this.

"What happened?" I said.

"The goddamn Department of goddamn Health, Education, and goddamn Welfare decided they didn't want to shell out two hundred thousand goddamn dollars for a Historic Whorehouse Shrine in Maine. They said we got the Henry Wadsworth Longfellow House—a lousy goddamn poet—and that's *enough!* That goddamn Gerald Ford, anyway—he's getting sneaky already!"

"What the hell has Ford got to do with it?"

"He's the Commander in Chief of the Army, isn't he? And Benedict Arnold was a general, wasn't he?"

"You mean there's a connection?"

"Of course! When Benedict Arnold went through Granby Lakes on his way to capture Quebec—way back in 1778—where do you suppose he slept?"

I couldn't resist the impulse to keep alive the legend I had created. "At the Honeymoon Mountain Inn, which was then the Sarah Selby cathouse, right?"

"You're goddamn right! That's what makes it historic!"

"I'll bet he was tired the next day," Bobby said.

"You're goddamn right he was. That's why he couldn't capture Quebec. You can't screw all night and fight the next day!"

I doubted this qualitative assumption, but I said nothing.

"I gotta call Muskie! He's just gotta pull some strings!" Egil Grimshaw said, slamming our front door off its hinges as he left.

If Senator Muskie pulled some strings, all it did was

make his pajamas fall down, because nothing else happened. If that. Reiko and I were back in the hotel business (much to the disappointment of the people of Granby Lakes) and had booked a convention of sixty-five honeymoon couples. "Different" honeymoon couples. They belonged to an organization called "The Over-Sixty Honeymoon Club," and that's exactly what it was—over-sixty couples who had just been married. They were delightful people, and although some of them had obviously been married before, and maybe many times, they acted as if this were their initial try. The night they arrived, none of them seemed to want to make the first move to go to bed. Poor Reiko was in the bar until three A.M., making all kinds of weird port and sherry drinks. Some of them drank nothing but warm milk, and it took a helluva long time for them to get high enough on warm milk to think about bed, let alone suggest it to their new spouses.

At about a quarter after three, I suggested maybe we'd all better turn in. This is apparently what they had been needing—a leader with some definite suggestions. All the blue-rinsed little old ladies coyly peeked over their little lace paper fans and giggled to their new husbands that they thought they'd get into something a little more comfortable and slipped shyly away to their respective rooms. The new husbands had "one for the road," whatever that could mean at their ages, and, in exactly seventeen minutes, left to join their cobwebby brides.

After this, Reiko dumped all the used glasses in the sink and sat down on a bar stool and lit a cigarette. (She was well into her third pack, despite the surgeon general.)

248

"They're pretty good drinkers," she said. "Made almost three hundred dollars tonight."

"On sherry and port and warm milk?"

"Sure—I've been giving the drinks all kinds of crazy names like the Banzai Boom-Boom, the Evel Knievel, the Doctor Feelgood—"

"The Doctor Feelgood? How do you make that?"

"Warm milk with a shot of Serutan. Serutan—that's 'Feelgood' spelled backwards."

I love Reiko, so I believed her.

CHAPTER

34

WITH our sixty-five "Over-Sixty Honeymooners," it looked as if we were going to make enough money to pay the town tax and the insurance—two very big gouging items in our budget—and maybe have a little left over to afford a treat of Twinkies once a month. By midmorning of their first full day, however, all our over-sixty honeymoon couples had moved out.

We learned this when we got back from a three-hour shopping tour "down to Rumford." There was a 1934 pickup truck parked in our driveway, and the front door was locked. After considerable pounding, the front door was opened by Filthy Phil, now dirtier, if possible, than he had been before. We had to back off from him. He smelled like the inside of a duck.

"Hey!" Filthy Phil shouted. He was glad to see us. "Where you been?"

"We've been shopping," I said. "And where is everybody?"

"Oh, we're all here. Place was kinda untidy when we got here. Buncha old farts running around like they owned the place—got 'em out quick. Just patted Old Betsy here, and they left pronto—that means 'quick.'"

"Papa," Bobby said, "Filthy Phil's got a shotgun. That's a shotgun he's carrying!" Bobby was sharp.

"Yep," Filthy Phil agreed, "Old Betsy here"—he patted the shotgun again—"people see her, they get the hell out fast."

"But," Reiko said, "those people were our hotel guests. We were going to make enough money to—Jack, call the sheriff!"

"I'm going to, right now," I said. "Get the hell out of the way with that shotgun!" Outrage gave me courage. Much to my surprise, Filthy Phil gave way, and even bowed as I passed him.

"Go right ahead," he said, "call the sheriff. Be my guest."

"What's that supposed to mean?" Reiko was very tense.

"Well," Phil said, standing up, stretching luxuriously and sharpening his toenails like an alley cat, on the leg of my favorite overstuffed chair, "there's been a little mistake. An honest mistake. A little misunderstanding. An honest misunderstanding—"

"Cut out the crap!" I yelled. "What's the mistake?"

"Well, when I signed that paper the other day, that paper you gave me—buying the place back. . . . The honest mistake is—I didn't have no right to sell it."

"You son of a bitch!" I said.

"You're certainly right about that," Filthy Phil said complacently, "you certainly are."

"What do you mean? And where's our thirty-five hundred dollars?" Reiko said.

"Well, the property was in my wife's name and she don't wanna sell it, and with your thirty-five hundred dollars, I done somethin' nice. I bought somethin'."

"I know what," Bobby said. "You bought another dead cow, right?"

Filthy Phil ignored this. "I did somethin' I've always wanted to do ever since we been married. They're havin' a big fancy dance down to the grange hall on Saturday night, so I went out and I bought a mink stole."

All of us were astonished.

"My God!" I said.

"Does your wife like it?" Reiko asked.

"Don't really matter if she does or she don't," Filthy said. *"I'm* the one who's goin' to the dance."

We had been *had*—by Egil Grimshaw, Joseph F. Fulman, Thomas E. Yates, The Granby Lakes Power Company, Judge Avon Bean, Elmer Dipple's garage, Harper Fundy's rigged Laundromat, Harriet Quimpy, Mark Tolland, the Titterford Hill Dairy, the state liquor board, the health inspector, the insurance broker, the state insurance bureau, the house painter, the plumbers, the electrician, the big enchiladas, and the small enchiladas—they had all taken us, but did we give up?

Read on.

‑

The man from the Interstate Moving and Storage Company of Strunkville was cooperative and also very sympathetic when we told him we had destroyed all the wardrobes, packing cases, and book boxes sold to us by United Van, and he showed a lot of compassion when he told us—quietly—in the family room of the Interstate Moving and Storage Company how much we would have to pay for new wardrobes, packing cases, and book boxes. Then he discreetly tippy-toed away and left us alone with our sorrow. It was like forest Lawn. They even had soft piped-in organ music, and a voice over, explaining, "The Lord giveth and the Lord taketh away."

Filthy Phil had graciously given us three days in which to "get the hell out," as he graciously put it. Reiko, Bobby, and I did the packing—helped no little, and I mean *no little* by Timothy. He just couldn't bear to see his thousands of toys being put into boxes without guarantee that he'd ever see them again. We were all a little crazy by the time we finished packing and the Interstate Moving van had pulled up at the front door.

We had, of course, planned to sue Egil Grimshaw for the fraudulent swindle he had pulled on us. I know that one of these words should be considered redundant, but not in our case. Also we knew it might take years or more to get any satisfactory settlement, so we were moving back to the blessed peace and quiet of the northern Ontario bush country, and if our kids couldn't get to school, maybe they'd learn something better, without all the pressures and prejudices and pettinesses of the so-called civilized world.

Dixey Bull, the head of Interstate Moving, was in

254

charge, and he and two not-so-willing workers loaded the van with all our worldly goods in a little less than six hours.

We had tried to remove our twenty dollar per yard wall-to-wall carpeting, but Filthy Phil demurred, patting Old Betsy for emphasis. I was all for getting my pistol (which I was allowed to carry because of large sums of money I was transporting—that's what it said on my permit, ho! ho! ho!) and blowing Filthy Phil's balls into the next county, but Reiko made me take a large glass of warm milk and a full box of Sominex and I sort of forgot the whole thing.

Even with all the grief and double-dealing and chicanery we had endured by owning the Honeymoon Mountain Inn, I felt a certain pang, a wrench, a touch of anguish at the thought of leaving this lovely place. A place in which we had put so much of our hearts, so much of our dreams, and, even in a short time, so much of our lives. And now we were leaving it all behind. I felt as if we were running away from something—a magic moment which we would never recapture.

Dixey and his two sluggish helpers climbed aboard the van, and Reiko, Bobby, Timothy, and I got into our old station wagon—this time with no screaming about who was going to sit where and "Fasten your safety belts, goddamnit!" None of us looked around for the last time. There was no point. And none of us noticed the deputy sheriff's car pulling up the driveway. Joey, the deputy sheriff, had an injunction, a *permanent* injunction obtained by Thomas E. Yates, the golf course owner. We could *never* use the driveway, our driveway, again. Not even to move the van and our car out and away? "No," Joey said. "If you ever use this driveway again, you will be in contempt of court and they'll throw you in jail!"

"I'll call Goldie Renk, my lawyer!" I screamed. I was out of control. On the verge of a complete breakdown.

"He already *knows* about it," Joey, the deputy, said. "He's the one who got the permanent injunction for Thomas E. Yates."

Joey, the deputy, got back into his car, and just as it started to snow, he saluted and drove off. "Have a nice weekend," he said.